The Contingent Self

The Contingent Self
One Reading Life

Virginia Brackett

Purdue University Press
West Lafayette, Indiana

Copyright © 2001 by Purdue University Press. All rights reserved.

05   04   03   02   01   5   4   3   2   1

The paper used in this book meets the minimum requirements of
American National Standard for Information Sciences—Permanence
of Paper for Printed Library Materials, ANSI Z39.48-1992.

Printed in the United States of America

Library of Congress Cataloging-in-Publication Data

Brackett, Virginia.
    The contingent self : one reading life / Virginia Brackett.
        p.   cm.
    Includes bibliographical references (p.) and index.
    ISBN 1-55753-223-0 (alk. paper)
    1. Brackett, Virginia.   2. Literature—History and criticism—
Theory, etc.   3. Literary historians—United States—Biography.
4. Critics—United States—Biography.   5. Books and reading.
6. Conduct of life. I. Title.
PS29.B7 A3 2001
809—dc21
[B]
                                                           2001019055

For Edmund C. Brackett:
unwaveringly supportive, mercifully parsimonious,
and fiercely devoted to the cause

Contents

Acknowledgments

I TAKE GREAT PLEASURE IN recognizing those to whom I incurred many debts while writing this book. I must first acknowledge the contributions of my dissertation committee chair, G. Douglas Atkins. His enthusiasm for this project from its inception both inspired and motivated me, while his honest assessment of matters intellectual and creative provided an unwavering guide to its completion. To additional committee members Margaret Arnold, Michael L. Johnson, Carolyn Doty and Chuck Marsh, I extend my gratitude for their abundant suggestions during the completion of my original manuscript and for their encouragement that I publish it. The administration of East Central University, in particular Duane Anderson, Vice President of Academic Affairs, deserves acknowledgment for its support of my pursuit of my doctorate and the writing of my dissertation during my early service there as Instructor of English.

I acknowledge the appearance of essay versions of Chapter One, "Sharp Necessities," in the fall 1996 issue of *Women & Language* (19.2: 7–13), and of Chapter Four, "Putting the Flowers In," in the June 2000 issue of *Arachnē: an Interdisciplinary Journal of the Humanities* (7.1:3–22). Their gracious release of publication rights is much appreciated.

The Contingent Self

Introduction

THIS WRITING PROJECT might be termed timely, in that, although late in coming, it came just in time. The personal criticism that follows represents not only a solution to a past problem, but a promise for my writing future. I pose in these chapters questions to readers only after excruciating and exacting consideration on my own part, and I openly celebrate the fact that many remain unanswered. That celebration symbolizes my liberation in that I no longer demand impossible answers from an unyielding world, but desire instead to engage that world in dialogue, a dialogue that produces its own brand of knowing. By employing tools of feminism, of postmodernism, and of personal experience, I seek scholarship and a positive audience response, but most of all, I seek satisfaction.

Here is how this part of my story began. After engaging in an exhausting and most unsatisfactory two-year struggle encompassing the production of three two-hundred-page attempts at a dissertation, I faced a major choice regarding my academic future. Try as I might, I simply could not produce that elusive written document that would allow me to claim the coveted doctoral degree. Unless I wanted to give up my doctoral pursuit altogether, a move I never seriously considered, I had to develop a plan. One option would be to start yet again, employing the same writing and research methodology, to construct a new version. But I had seen no illuminating scrawls on the wall, experienced no epiphany that promised another effort would represent any

1

improvement. A second option would be to abandon that dissertation project and begin anew, and I tried repeatedly to seriously consider that new beginning. But no matter how gingerly I approached the idea, it skittered away like a gun-shy rabbit. I felt locked into some crazy mental choreography with the writing project serving as my mismatched partner. With a marked lack of grace, we repeated the same tired steps, never achieving the rhythm essential to a well-executed dance.

Although my vita reflected the publication of four articles in academic journals, approximately one hundred articles and stories in various popular periodicals, one young adult biography for library distribution featuring a woman Renaissance writer, and two contracts for additional nonfiction books, my written expression in the dissertation pleased neither me nor my committee. These committee members were not nameless faces; I knew them as individuals, and the majority conducted classes I had attended in which all awarded me good marks on course papers, even when they offered a plethora of suggestions for future revision. Yet now I received comments on my dissertation drafts such as "your categories need clearer definition"; "look at your list [of similarities between Elizabeth Cary and Anne Bradstreet] again and consider whether or not a point adds anything"; "[i]f you keep Bradstreet, I think that the Ralegh material has promise; maybe you can improve the discussion of du Bartas, if you really think about it and organize more clearly"; "your problem in knowledge is related to the fuzziness of your controlling ideas"; "I'm sure you've worked hard on this new version, which I can see differs considerably from the previous one but . . ."; "think more productively about the participation of women writers in contemporary literary discourses and cultural debates"; and "your study fails to engage meaningfully [fill in the blank]." I had gathered decent research, and a few sections of what I'd begun to call, not without affection, "the monster," appeared quite strong, but obviously my writing style and organizational skills remained lacking. As for those fuzzy ideas, I could no longer chalk them up to a late-night caffeine buzz; something was definitely amiss.

I had encountered this problem with my writing before, and I attributed it then to a certain writing schizophrenia I suffered due to my interests in writing for both a popular and an academic audience. Each demands its own particular style and approach, and I'm sure that I sometimes confuse the two. That confusion, however, paled by comparison to my bafflement when I shared with a professor whom I admire my brief article that suggested a little-known seventeenth-century advice treatise on breast feeding by Elizabeth Knevet Clinton as source matter for Anne Bradstreet. Although the article had been accepted by a well-recognized journal, he returned it to me covered with inked corrections and suggestions. These comments accompanied his note of congratulations, tempered with a caution that the journal surely would never print an article that poorly written. The journal's editors requested no revision, and the article appeared verbatim a few months later.

I'd had much experience with this kind of subjectivity regarding publication in the popular market. Rejection or acceptance of popular writing seemed to be determined at times simply by an editor's success or failure during her weekend golf game and her resultant mood. On three different occasions, stories or articles I thought perfect for particular periodicals suffered rejection, but when I resubmitted six months later, all of them were purchased and subsequently appeared in print. But the evidence of such subjectivity in the judgment of writing within academia startled me. I had been encouraged to believe there existed an obviously clear and correct approach to academic writing by the comments on my dissertation efforts. The incident further eroded my already diminished self-confidence as well as my confidence in the system on which my future depended.

Over a six-month period following the last receipt of comments on my dissertation, I at last forced my reluctant self to consider its future carefully, but I could summon no optimism regarding a project once fiercely pursued. Just as my fingers edged toward the panic button, a solution presented itself, as solutions often will, at an unexpected moment from a most trustworthy and insightful source. A comment from my husband succeeded in jump-starting the thought processes I had paralyzed by my own depleted self-assurance. The common occurrence of such interchanges throughout our relationship should have mitigated my surprise, but the accuracy of his thought stunned me. A great one for reductive statement, he said during a lengthy conversation about my dissertation, "It seems to me that you're not using your writing strengths." He remains the master of the classical understatement.

In one of those rare moments of great clarity, I realized the simple truth in his words. For two years I had toiled to present a shining example of traditional formal research in a collection of objective articles, all the while chafing beneath the constraints connected to such expression. As time passed, my confusion over the development of what appeared to be my growing ineptness escalated. My publication record should have assured me that I could perform some type of writing satisfactorily. While I clung stubbornly to much of the subject *matter* of my dissertation, the time had arrived to temporarily dismiss the *manner* of academic writing that so frustrated me. I rejected its demand for what I felt to be an awkwardly restrained objectivity in the presentation of research so personal and vital to my life. I chose, rather, to embrace the method I most appreciated, that of personal criticism.

Three years earlier, graduate school had offered a single opportunity for me to gain experience in this type of writing through a personal criticism writing seminar. The seminar, given by G. Douglas Atkins, a great proponent of this mode of professional expression, left me breathless with relief and delight as I explicated in a lengthy paper those personal issues the study of Renaissance writer Elizabeth Cary allowed me to challenge. The paper—Atkins prefers the term "essay"—featured information about Cary's works as well as references to feminist criticism, a mode of criticism to which I had taken like the proverbial desperately dry duck. I had a story to tell, a story personal yet all too common in our society, and Elizabeth Cary provided its foundation. Study of her persistence in writing, and making public her writing, during a time when such activity on the part of women enjoyed scant encouragement; learning of her personal struggle with religious faith leading to her conversion to Catholicism at a time when such conversion on the part of anyone could cause dire consequences; learning that this declaration of faith caused her husband of twenty years to remove their children from her care and to convince Charles I to place her under house arrest; coming to believe that she authored an extraordinary history of Edward II for which she still has not fully received credit—all of these factors meant, and mean, far more to me than their representation as mere facts and issues in a textbook. The personal critical essay provided the venue for expressing that "far more" aspect. At last I could share not only what I had learned from Elizabeth Cary, but how and why that learning had changed my outlook on life.

After surviving a mental battle of pro versus con, and a careful measure of political risks and the state of my sanity, I contacted Professor Atkins, who also happened to be my graduate advisor. Stifling my hubris, I remained fully prepared to beg and plead that he assume the chairpersonship of a new committee, and that he approve my change in dissertation approach. My joy and relief exceeded all bounds when he immediately agreed. Shortly thereafter, this collection of closely-related personal critical writings took shape.

Coincidental to my renewing my dissertation efforts, my husband had, in anticipation of his own dissertation, cajoled me into reviewing my exposure to postmodern thought and methodology through deconstruction and poststructuralism. What I recalled of these critical applications and their connection to matters post-modern I reluctantly shared, but that was not a great deal. Jacques Derrida, Michel Foucault and Jean-François Lytoard I found frankly depressing during my brief exposure to their ideas in the beginning years of my graduate studies. Their suggestion that words did not mean what they seemed to mean and their lambasting of those epistemes or metanarratives I held so dear threatened my most basic sensibilities. I wanted badly to believe that some approach to the defining of reality, whether that of science, religion, or something else, held promise for the discovery of Truth with a capital "T." Postmodern ideas threatened that desire. But in realizing the shallow quality of my knowledge about such topics, I allowed my initial resistance to evolve into a cautious interest, particularly as my husband discussed with me his discoveries of recent commentary on postmodern thought.

While inhabiting the sixteenth and seventeenth centuries for the previous five years, I had successfully managed to shut out many of the developments within the postmodern approach. This, I now acknowledged, was a mistake, for some ideas of post-modernism, particularly those reflected by poststructuralism, obviously intersect with feminist concerns. Indeed, a review of these intersections helped clarify for me the problems encountered by many feminist writers in approaching traditional academic writing. How marvelous, I thought, that all these centuries later, long after Horace declared literature's aim to be *dulce et utile,* literature continues to, as Sir Philip Sidney put it, delight *and* teach. That I might discover a solution to my problems encountered in writing about seventeenth-century Renaissance women through examination of contemporary critical theory and postmodern thought reaffirmed my confidence in the eternal nature of literature; it was just a "nature" I had to re-envision. A postmodern approach encourages this dissolving of distinctions and allows a movement away from universal standards seen in a literature canon that values exclusivity. Those metanarratives to which I so stubbornly clung, and the knowledge, beliefs, and practices they legitimated, were still of value to me in my study and writing. Detrimental, however, was the marginalization, by that same process of legitimization, of most of the women's writing that captivated me.

My new interest in postmodern thought broadened along with my reading. The elusive character of postmodern philosophy makes its definition impossible, for defining, in the traditional sense of the term, flies in the face of the postmodern approach. Postmodernism, then, problematizes its own definition. Lyotard offers as his definition of postmodernism "an incredulity toward metanarratives" (xxiv), eventually suggesting that postmodernism remains under constant redefinition: "the emphasis can be placed on the powerlessness of the faculty of presentation, on the nostalgia for presence felt by the human subject, on the obscure and futile will which inhabits him in spite of everything" (79). He suggests that what challenges our beliefs and ideas at one moment, in the next may become what we attempt to challenge. This concept goes a long way to speaking my own confusion at this shifting point in my engagement of literature and life.

As each interested individual must, I constructed a working definition of postmodernism for myself, beginning with those things that postmodern thought does *not* do. The postmodern approach avoids reductionism, rejects grand narratives that privilege only certain points of view in favor of more localized accounts, and avoids word games that support particular power structures. Once I identify what postmodern thought declines, I focus on what it examines. Its embracing of the concept of a historically constructed truth, based on myths of legitimization, offers a fine tool for one bearing the burden of reconstructing, rewriting, her own history. A jarring midlife change that re moved me from my role of wife and mother brought with it the shocking realization that the person I had been was a construct compliments of others. Postmodern thought bolsters my courage for the task at hand: reconstruction of self-identity.

Now I can springboard into a consideration of deconstruction, which tells me that the thing signified through language, for example woman, is not of most importance. That importance belongs to the signifier, to all those various meanings embedded in that picture we draw as w-o-m-a-n; it becomes capable of assigning meaning and even substance on its own. The signifier can be the signified as well, and language loses the modernist's promise that we can look through it to a truth beyond (Atkins and Johnson, 6). Neither reading nor writing, as suggested by David Kaufer and Gary Waller, represents an "unmediated, straightforward" activity; rather these activities are "culturally acquired, 'unnatural' activities" (67). To this idea I add that of Gayatri Chakravorty Spivak, who explains that "the world actually writes itself with the many-leveled, unfixable intricacy and openness of a work of literature" (27). Vincent B. Leitch tells us that all "writing is understood, in the widest possible sense, to include all forms of inscription, ranging from carving a path through a forest to recalling a dream to penning a legal code" (23). He offers several statements I remember finding applicable to my teaching of composition in the past that refresh my memory of deconstructive ideas. Leitch advises us to be ever-mindful of the constitution of all knowledge "during a certain time by one or two people"(22). The powers behind this constitution exclude certain "things" that don't work well to complement their modernist vision. Thus, "our knowledge, in its present and past formations and branches, could have been, and may yet be, constituted in other ways. Our relation to 'facts,' disciplines, departments, and hierarchies of knowledge is less 'natural' or 'normal' than it is concocted and thus alterable" (23). I have already been engaged in a deconstruction of my own history, concocted for me by others, exulting in the alterable quality that deconstruction reveals.

In her study *Foucault Feminism*, Lois McNay explains that "the poststructuralist philosophical critique of the rational subject has resonated strongly with the feminist critique of rationality as an essentially masculine construct" (2). Her statement means to me that poststructuralism reveals the traditionally *rational* objective approach to academic writing as constructed by males as the only type of writing granted professional status by academe. The problem (for certain men) with that idea is that academe no longer remains an exclusively male bastion. McNay adds, "Moreover, feminists have drawn extensively on the poststructuralist argument that rather than having a fixed core or essence, subjectivity is constructed through language and is, therefore, an open-ended, contradictory and culturally specific amalgam of different subject positions" (2). Because my "subject position," that of a female in a patriarchal society, differs vastly from that of those patriarchs who lay down the rules of behavior for that society, I may not be able comfortably to assume their approach to, or attitude toward, any particular aspect of life and living. Nor, in my opinion and that of McNay, should I be expected to. The essay, rather than the masculinized article, offers an opportunity to write the way my subject position has prepared me to write. As Atkins says, "the essay is, it seems to me, nonphallocentric and so is the kind of writing best suited to an open, humane teaching such as that sought by feminists" (15).

Postmodern thought agrees with that of feminism on a further point that applies also to the writing of personal literary criticism. Part of the difficulty women writers encounter in their work remains tied to our culture's encouragement that all individuals search for that essential and supposedly coherent self discussed as the basis for self-identity by modern psychology. Again, we're talking about theory composed *by* men and basically *about* men. When Freud, for instance, wrote about women, he approached them as lesser humans lacking the male aspect of the penis: castrated men, in effect. His ideas reflect those of a medieval viewpoint that sees women as incomplete males. Women, then, are less-than-ideal humans, flawed in a physical and, consequently, also a spiritual and emotional sense. Leaders of Western culture even doubted that women possessed souls well into the beginnings of the English Renaissance. So now, because women, in asking "Who am I?," cannot participate in the male assumption that "an *a priori* . . . ultimate unity and fixity of being" exists, Patricia Waugh suggests they would better ask, "'*What* am I?'" (10, emphasis added). Waugh explains that "this question carries an implicit and necessary recognition of alienation: the phenomenological perception that 'I' am never at one with myself because always and ever already constituted by others according to whom, and yet outside of what, I take myself to be" (10–11). Women are not men, yet they have through the ages been defined, designed, and refined by men. Tools of feminism aid in my understanding that my ideas about myself have been shaped by others; I play Galatea to Western culture's Pygmalion. As one of those tools, personal criticism allows me to ask "Who am I?" and to investigate the myriad answers that arise.

While some feminists see postmodern ideas as threatening the success of the political movement that grew from their ideologies, others regard postmodern thought as a boon. Janice McLaughlin summarizes the arguments for both views, well-formulated in a multitude of criticism, in her article "Feminist Relations with Postmodernism," which offers an understandable explanation of points of dispute, but also suggests that feminists' fear of postmodernism is unfounded. In her opinion postmodern thought will not purloin "something essential to the success and capabilities of feminism," nor will it reduce feminism "to an esoteric mind-game of little importance" (6–7) to those outside academia. She basically argues against the idea that postmodern thought steals from feminism its analytical tools and its distinctive voice and ideology. I must agree with her, in that postmodern thought lays no special claim to truth; it declares frankly that laying claim to truth is not its aim. And it certainly does not compete with critical theory, such as feminism, an approach that often employs the use of the first person and reflects "the belief that the researcher cannot be removed/separated from his/her research nor the author from her/his narrative" (Tierney, 7).

Like McLaughlin, I do not view postmodernism as intent upon the exclusion of women or any other marginalized group; rather, from my vantage point, a postmodern approach encourages in particular the acceptance of literature and criticism by women. I do believe that complaints about postmodernism's original, largely European-based ideas being grounded in the privileged position of patriarchy is valid; it adopts males both as its focus in a study of subjectivity and as its most prolific voices. But in America, to which McLaughlin refers as "the home of individualism," the voice of Richard Rorty serves to counteract such claims. In Rorty's writings, I find the crucial point McLaughlin also offers: postmodernism has not necessarily entered feminism as a privileged approach, a favorite child so to speak, that wants to force feminists to surrender "the particular struggles which flow from the significantly different historical position of women" (McLaughlin, 9). The umbrella of postmodernism covers many approaches, as does that of feminism. One postmodern approach exists that is less "relevant to the supposed masters of postmodernism, less concerned with the purities of theoretical ideas," and much more focused and "driven" by "the different positions of women." This approach rests on two vital premises. The first is that of *contingency,* the importance of viewing all things in relation to all others. The second stresses *agency,* or the power to act, offered by solidarity, a banding together of beings who share common beliefs. Rorty considers both contingency and solidarity crucial to a satisfying human existence.

An important aspect of Rorty's postmodern ideas is the acceptance of the proposition that questions of difference must be addressed, not ignored. Those questions relate to gender, class, race, economics, religion—the multitude of differences that make us at once dissimilar and interesting. It also acknowledges that "the practice of questioning and highlighting contingency did not enter feminism through postmodernism but through activism" (McLaughlin, 9). This is a point on which Rorty agrees. Postmodern ideas are just that—ideas, not a blueprint for political or social agency. Postmodern thought has, however, served to support identification of those social constructs, or metanarratives, upon which women's ideas of self remain contingent.

I should make clear that while McLaughlin's discussion relates directly to aspects of Rorty's discussion of postmodernism, the identification of her ideas with his remains my own, for she never mentions him. Considered America's foremost philosopher by many, Rorty bears watching. I find especially interesting that he resigned a position as professor of philosophy at Princeton to assume a professorship in humanities at the University of Virginia. As I read more of Rorty's writing, I understand that literature remains a vital part of his life and a personal tool for his understanding of himself and those who make up his world. This allows me to feel at least a partial solidarity of my own, for the first time, with a recognized expert in postmodern thought.

McLaughlin's most valuable point in relation to Rorty's ideas begins with her statements about ideas of subjecthood in general. She reminds us that a fundamental point in the consideration of the state of subjecthood "is the belief that the subject is autonomous, a free thinking rational being, in control of who and what they are, and fully cognizant of the reality they live within" (10). Marginalized groups, such as women and racial minorities, protest rightly that such a belief can apply only to whatever group within a culture happens to hold power. From an elite chosen few, in our culture usually white males, subjectivity allows the flow of political agency in which an "autonomous agent" may act in his or her behalf. McLaughlin labels a combination of the two areas of thought I have been discussing as the single unit "feminism and postmodernism," then shows how the unit questions "the possibility of anyone being in the above sense autonomous and rational" (10). I like that approach, because even those who retain economic and/or political power in a culture are constantly challenged by events and conditions beyond their control. McLaughlin's feminism and postmodernism combine in seeing subjecthood as "transitory, contingent, and relational to context and power" (11). She refers to individual humans as "social actors," reminding me of Shakespeare's "poor player / who struts and frets his hour upon the stage" (*Macbeth*, 5.5.24–25), a shadow life without control over its elements. The importance of this lack of autonomy on the part of any subject also illuminates my preference for writing that reflects all the different forces acting on me as I write. This method of writing, like McLaughlin's feminism and postmodernism, recognizes that "subjecthood is inseparable from the life that [humans] lead, that life is inseparable from a multiplicity of forces and movements which they come in contact with, each with an interrelated norm of agency, behavior and signification" (11).

Rorty's book *Contingency, Irony and Solidarity* supports this very point in a lucid presentation that employs literature and writers as examples. A particularly useful discussion for any member of a marginalized group who has ever suffered emotional abuse is Rorty's overview of cruelty as it relates to the undermining of solidarity. He uses as a framework George Orwell's novel *1984* (1948). Before I read far into his discussion, I pause to think of what I remember about Orwell's novel. The word *control* naturally comes to mind, and the loss of freedom due to Big Brother, an idea that found its way into so many phrases as humanity reached the late twentieth century.

Sure enough, as I read on, Rorty confirms Orwell's anticipation of socialization's reductionary effect on the individual. Rorty writes pertaining to solidarity that people consist only of "what has been socialized into them—their ability to use language, and thereby to exchange beliefs and desires with other people" (177). This type of programmed exchange, whereby we trade with others ideas that are not really our own, prevents true solidarity. If individuals simply echo cultural propaganda, they come together on a false basis created by someone or something outside themselves, apart from their real desires. This makes impossible honest, personal interaction as a basis for the small sharing communities that Rorty projects as the answer to a search for reality. Such communities may exist only if the individual looks beyond her/his basis of socialization to imagine an alternative approach to self-realization.

I further personalize this idea, envisioning a lack of solidarity with one's own self, should that self undergo coercion to adopt another's values or approach to life. Such coercion or pressure to conform to an idea not our own clearly represents abuse of our humanity. If socialization remains based upon such an abusive relationship at any point in life, one's subjectivity is vulnerable to the party in power.

❧

A horrendous midlife occurence forced the personal changes responsible for my discovery of the promise of feminist analysis, both political and critical. Among other alterations, it caused my swing from conservative politics to those of the cautiously liberal and a rejection of the devoted practice of organized religion in favor of a spirituality based on personal belief rather than external edict. These changes occurred not overnight, for I was a reluctant convert, having believed practically from birth in those very metanarratives in which Lyotard encourages incredulity. After serving in the prescribed role of wife for eighteen years, suddenly I became a single parent. Without time to regain balance or orientation, I was, with malice aforethought on the part of another, sucked into an abysmal cavern of loss by the legal withdrawal of the custody of three children, due to no fault of my own. These emotional and psychological upheavals forced an acknowledgment that my lifelong support system had failed and failed dismally. If ever anyone stood ready for the support feminism yields, I was that person.

Yet I resisted this support. Long entrenched in the nightmarish world of patriarchal marriage and vocation, escape for me proved difficult. This one fact may have been the hardest for me to accept; the least of Earth's creatures will move away from a pain-inflicting agent, yet I had found such a move impossible, causing irreparable damage not only to myself but also to others. My inaction caused almost as much pain as the events following my decision to change my circumstances. Even after adjusting somewhat to my new life and all of its losses and gains, I still wondered why I hesitated all those years to take protective action. Now, years later, this writing project helps me grasp the reason behind my slow emergence from a detrimental environment. A study and discussion of Rorty's brand of postmodernism, its ideas standing side by side with those of feminism, allows clarification of my situation. His discussion of cruelty, as it relates to Orwell's novel, is part of that study.

Rorty comments that Orwell "sensitized his [readers] to a set of excuses for cruelty which had been put into circulation by a particular group—the use of the rhetoric of 'human equality' by intellectuals who had allied themselves with a spectacularly successful criminal gang" (171). In the last part of his novel Orwell focuses, however, not on totalitarian states, but on the character Smith and his torture. While Orwell was not original in suggesting the takeover of modern states by technologically astute gangsters, according to Rorty he "was the first to ask how intellectuals in such states might conceive of themselves, once it had become clear that liberal ideals had no relation to a possible human future" (171). Subjectivity would become a matter of slavery that involved a loss of imagination to some politically formulated idea of goodness put forth by those who controlled culture.

Rorty explains that humiliation is evident through Smith's total denial of self; he bends to his manipulators and agrees aloud that "two plus two equals five," contradicting all logic and his own belief. Such humiliation, according to Rorty, remains the ultimate sadistic manipulation that one human may inflict upon another, for "sadism aims at humiliation rather than merely at pain in general" (177). Abuse of this type can produce a psychological and emotional pain so intense, it defies description. Even now, as I think of instances from my own life, my throat constricts and an unpleasant tingling takes hold of my neck, like that caused by contact with chilled fingers. I notice my breathing grows shallow and measured, the slowing metabolism of an organism cautious and under siege. Humiliation, inflicted through verbal attack, by a figure one wants to respect or love, causes a peculiar shrinking down into the dark areas of one's self. It provokes a futile search for a hiding place that simply does not exist this side of insanity.

Rorty agrees with Elaine Scarry that the initial infliction of agony is secondary in effect to the later use of that same agony in such a way that a subject "cannot reconstitute herself" once the immediate abuse ceases: "The idea is to get her to do or say things—and, if possible, believe and desire things, think thoughts—which later she will be unable to cope with having done or thought. . . . [Y]ou [make] it impossible for her to use *contingency* language to describe what she has been" (177–78). When one person forces another to act in a way she finds despicable, he manipulates her into a first step toward disbelieving in her own selfhood; "she becomes incapable of weaving a coherent web of belief and desire" (178). These behaviors may force the victim to question her most sacred beliefs. How can she hold onto ideals she values when she has acted in a way that contradicts those very ideals? When she steps back to view those actions, as an objective third person might, they reflect a denial of her own convictions. Naturally, such a perception makes her "irrational. She is unable to give a reason for her belief that fits together with her other beliefs. She becomes irrational not in the sense that she has lost contact with reality but in the sense that she can no longer rationalize—no longer justify herself to herself" (178). These ideas, or something closely akin to them, I had already discovered in feminist theory.

<hr />

A study of literature during the process of my metamorphosis helped ease my transition. A long-postponed admission of identification with the many female victims around me also helped, and a final embracing of feminist ideology at last liberated me to the point that I recognized I need not burden myself alone with the crushing responsibility for the chaos that was representing my life. This process that so obsessed and possessed me, a direct result of my graduate studies, could not sensibly be separated from my academic writing, at least not in every instance. I agree with Nancy Miller, who, in speaking specifically of the particularly helpful use of metaphor in personal criticism, but supporting more generally personal criticism itself, writes, "perhaps what seems most 'feminist' to me about the uses of both metaphor and narrative criticism is the self-consciousness these modes of analysis tend to display about their own processes of theorization; a self-consciousness that points to the fictional strategies inherent in all theory" (xii).

Hardly the rebellious type by nature, I never sought to play David versus the Goliath of the traditional, objective, linear writing inherent in my academic training. I just longed for something more, something to allow expression of that continuous restructuring of self that I believed to be the purpose of education. Confinement of such an approach to the margins of academic writing seems nothing less than discrimination. It suggests an effort by the powers who define and maintain "standards" within academe in pursuit of the so-called maintenance of excellence to support a status quo. That status quo, exclusionary in nature, undermines "feminine epistemic authority" (Frey, 45).

This collection of personal criticism, then, while elaborating, partly through the use of postmodern ideas, on the feminist view of the traditional patriarchal approach to academic writing, pleads not for its disappearance, but instead acts as a supportive voice in the argument for the inclusion and legitimizing of the personal critical essay within academe. Like Atkins, who maintains he has no desire "to replace the article with the essay" (15), and others who have addressed this issue, I simply present a challenge to this "preferred mode for discussion." I hope that my writing also will serve to "question the importance of the objective and impersonal" while avoiding a "seamless, finished 'product'" in deference to writings that make "direct reference to the process" through which they developed (Freedman, Frey, and Zauhar, 2–3).

Great support continues to gather in favor of personal criticism, including its acceptance by a slowly increasing number of academic journals. For example, the first chapter that appears here, "Sharp Necessities," created in Atkins's seminar mentioned above, appeared in the 1996 winter edition of *Women & Language,* published by George Mason University. One would hope that eventually Olivia Frey's desire that our "profession 'open up' and provide writers with 'more freedom to write about literature in alternative forms and . . . [to] be rewarded by it: the dissertation topics supported, the articles published; the writers hired, tenured, promoted'" (Freedman, Frey, and Zauhar, 4) will become routine rather than revolutionary. Like other feminist demands, this one likely faces a lengthy rite of passage before acceptance. When one considers historical attitudes toward female intelligence versus that of males, the delayed endorsement of methods and techniques growing from feminism is understandable—understandable, but not necessarily acceptable. As Jane Tompkins and others put it, the epistemology, or methods used in the process of understanding knowledge, of our Western culture is influenced by a belief that emotion has no place within that process. Women are viewed as stereotypically emotional and intuitive; therefore, emotion and intuition are second-rate approaches to knowledge. "Because women in our culture are not simply encouraged but *required* to be the bearers of emotion, which men are culturally conditioned to repress," such an epistemology neatly omits women and women's ways of knowing from the intellectual loop (25–26).

I recall seeing this epistemology beautifully expressed by Hélène Cixous in a reading I encountered early in graduate studies. She writes of the classic man/woman opposition, one of those binaries that deconstruction reveals, that it "automatically means great/small, superior/inferior . . . means high or low, means Nature/history, means transformation/inertia . . . the difference between active/passive" (44). Some time was required before I could apply words like these to myself, to my own desires and pursuits. Tentatively, I began substituting the word *I* for the word *she*, my own name for the word *woman*, in the feminist writings I encountered. At last aroused from my postdomestic dissolution stupor, I found that identification with descriptions from women writers like Cixous helped in my attempts at social repositioning. I could locate meaning based on personal experience in passages describing "woman" like the following from Cixous: "Without man she would be indefinite, indefinable, nonsexed, unable to recognize herself; outside the symbolic. But fortunately there is man . . . who teaches her to be aware of lack, to be aware of absence, aware of death. It's man who will finally order woman, 'set her to rights' by teaching that . . . 'without me you wouldn't exist'" (46). I discovered, with no small amount of joy, that I could unlearn such instruction through the aid of literature, the study and application of ideas from a postmodern era and feminist criticism and critique, and the writing such study and my life experiences inspired.

My firm belief that a combination of these elements not only works but works splendidly stands behind my writing of personal criticism. In addition to the obvious therapeutic value any writing affords, this particular approach to the discussion of literature lends itself to sharing with a popular, as well as an academic, audience, extending its value, both therapeutic and intellectual. This extension I envision as an important aspect of the academic experience. Having been so long a member of that popular reading audience before joining that of the academic, I retain faith in its ability to digest and benefit from discoveries that academics tend to hoard. There exists no reasonable explanation for the necessity some scholars see in withholding certain of the results of literary study from that other group, unless it be a reluctance to write with the clarity necessary to make digestible and enjoyable the fruits of their education by more than a tiny and exclusive readership. Such a reluctance, to my mind, indicates a snobbery both unprofessional and born of an overrated sense of self-importance.

The following examples of personal criticism stand as testimony to my belief that academia should not only embrace but also encourage a number of approaches to self-expression on the part of its scholars. Only then will it escape enslavement to an epistemology every bit as confining and controlling as the metanarratives postmodern commentators ask us to regard with a healthy suspicion. When enthusiasts of traditional patriarchal writing proclaim that theirs is the only path to Truth, this represents a dangerous echo of the sort once insisting that the distant flat horizon indicated a flat planet. The defining of reality remains a slippery and confounding activity at best; we should approach it with caution, but also with a sense of adventure and a joy in expression promoting pleasure as a crucial aspect of professionalism.

CHAPTER ONE

Sharp Necessities

March 24, 1627

My Lord, I received yesterday from your Lordship . . . an expression of his Majesty's pleasure. . . . It is to command me to my mother's in the nature of a prisoner. . . . I have committed no fault that I know of, and though I had, sure I believe the King would take some other way of punishment, than so unusual a one as to starve me to death. . . . I, therefore, desire that . . . your Lordship will be pleased, in compassion of a woman distressed without just cause, to move his Majesty for me: and if it may please him to have me removed from London, it is my most earnest desire, if my Lord will give me necessary means to feed and clothe me, for nothing keeps me here but sharp necessity.[1]

—A daughter of Elizabeth Cary,
The Lady Falkland, Her Life

I N THE FALL OF 1991, having received my initial assignment in my first seminar in the doctoral program at the University of Kansas, I enter the Spencer Research Library. This will be the first of many steps in my subsequent search for information regarding Elizabeth Cary. At that moment, I know her only as the mysterious "E. F.," sometime-author of an obscure history of Edward II written during the Renaissance.

"I'm looking," I tell the librarian, "for a book written in seventeenth-century England, probably by a woman named

Elizabeth Cary." Glancing at the note I clutch in my hand, I add, "That could be spelled C-a-r-y or C-a-r-e-y or C-a-r-e-w."

When his eyebrows ascend one notch, I rush to continue, "But it could be listed under her husband's name, Henry Falkland." I hand him my scribbling and point out a set of initials, "E. F." "My professor says these are all that appear on the book by way of an author's name. He thinks the book is here in the Rare Books Collection."

He considers, then leads me first to the card catalogue. When we discover nothing listed under the various spellings of "Cary" that matches my notes, we consult *The National Union Catalogue*, again striking out. Next we try *The Short Title Catalogue*.

"*The History of King Edward II*," he reads from the index. "No Elizabeth Cary/Carey/Carew listed here, nor," he pauses to consult my note again, "any Elizabeth Falkland. But there are a few gentlemen's names. Let's see. Yes, Falkland, Henry Cary, first Viscount." Armed with this new information, we find the card catalogue to be more accommodating. We discover the Viscount Falkland's name on a card listing the history in question: Item E129.

Moments later, I stare briefly at the cover of E129 before opening what will be my private Pandora's box for the remainder of my student career and well into my professional life. I read: *The History of the Life, Reign, and Death of Edward II, King of England, and Lord of Ireland. With the Rise and Fall of his great Favourites, Gaveston and the Spencers. Written by E. F. in the year 1627. And Printed verbatim from the original.*

My gaze falls to a handwritten note on the inside page of the book that reads:

By Henry Cary Lord Viscount Falkland who died 1633. He was father of Lucius Cary Viscount Falkland who was killed Sept 1643 at the battle of Newberg fighting for Charles 1st. This book was found amongst the papers of Henry Cary Lord Falkland after his death and was published as his in 1680 when it was the fashion to say anything that could be said against the government of Charles II.

—Anthony Wood (signature).

I sit back to consider. No wife, no Elizabeth, mentioned. My eyes return to the notation, "written by E.F." Surely these initials stand for Elizabeth Falkland. I read on, next digesting the author's direct address to his/her reader.

20 Feb. 1627

To out-run those weary hours of a deep and sad Passion, my melancholy Pen fell accidentally on the Historical Relation; which speaks a King, our own though one of the most Unfortunate, and shews the Pride and Fall of his inglorious Minions. I have herein followed the dull Character of our Historians, nor amplified more than they infer, by Circumstance. I strive to please the Truth, not Time, nor fear I Censure, since at the worst, 'twas but one month mis-spended; which cannot promise ought in right Perfection. If so you hap to view it, tax not my Errours; I my self confess them. E. F.

A deep and sad passion? I pause, struck by the graceful candor of this phrase; a warm empathy stirs within. Later I read that Cary supposedly wrote the history during an enforced separation from her husband and children, what amounted to house arrest. Lord Falkland, furious over his wife's secret conversion to Catholicism, removed her from his presence and her children from her care. Such emotional upheaval could account for the plaintive phrase. But for centuries the history remained under Falkland's name, because of its discovery among his possessions. Only recently has the authorship been questioned, and now mounting evidence supports the claim for Cary's authorship. Not everyone remains convinced, as my difficulty in locating the book has proven. "The gender bias dictating the attribution to Viscount Falkland persists in library entries," Barbara Lewalski states (317). Overcoming such bias proves difficult when claims lack the support of absolute authenticity. In the absence of such proof, critics must look to other methods by which to substantiate their claims, so that Donald A. Stauffer, for instance, "ventured a hesitant attribution to Elizabeth Cary on grounds of dramatic scenic elements and style" (317).[2]

I ponder Stauffer's hint at something peculiarly feminine in the writing of *Edward II,* a point upon which feminist critics apparently base their support of Cary's authorship. Feminist critics? At that time, the term still evoked for me images of Gloria Steinem and a few of my bra-burning sorority sisters of the 70s. Once, touched by the fever of social consciousness, even I attended the local drive-in sans brassiere. The fact that my escort of the evening failed to notice my personal drama did little to diminish my self-satisfaction. Can such scenes possibly relate to Cary's text?

Lewalski claims that internal clues, including "the dramatic scenes and speeches, the feminist portrait of Queen Isabel, and the sympathetic treatment of the Pope and the Catholic clergy— inconceivable from the rabidly antipapist Falkland" (319) support argument favoring Cary's authorship. Details from the history can be "usefully contextualized with reference to the circumstances of [Cary's] own life," circumstances including "the clash of authorities claiming her obedience. . . . All her life Cary seems to have been caught up in conflict between social and ideological pressures to conform and submit, and an inner imperative to resist and challenge authority" (181).

I subsequently discover that Renaissance ideology concerning women was based, in part, upon an ancient view (Aristotle's) of biology, later supported by Galen. "A female was by nature a defective male," lacking the heat to extrude her genitals in the manner of the male's. "The matter she contributes to generation, the menses, lacks 'the principle of soul'; this [is] contributed only by the male" (Jordan, 30–31). Her cool and damp "humors" meant the female possessed a deceptively changeable temperament. Most feminine ills could be categorized as hysteria (the root *hyster* being Greek for *womb*). One Renaissance writer noted, "Her womb was like a hungry animal; when not amply fed by sexual intercourse or reproduction, it was likely to wander about her body, overpowering her speech and senses" (Davis, 147–48). "My God," I mutter, thinking of my own daughters. What kind of a self-image could possibly grow from such ideas? Having choked down the wandering-womb theory, I allow my attention to be claimed by an issue less metaphysical. Betty Travitsky tells us that "the *feme* [sic] *covert* (married woman) had no public rights . . . and no redress under law for physical, economic, or social brutalization by her husband" (185). So sat Cary, abandoned and misplaced, the "*feme covert*" incarnate. How might she feel to know her thirty days "mis-spended" sparked an authorship debate centuries later?

I reflect upon my own previous month mis-spended, recalling the nasty court battle waged over the custody of my three children. I had watched my life unravel over the previous few weeks after my ex-husband, who shared joint legal custody of our daughters and son, refused to give me permission to move the children out of state, a move necessitated by my continuing education. He informed me that I had no reason to pursue further education: my original degree should earn me a living. That original degree in medical technology I chose twenty years earlier due to our imminent marriage. Eschewing my love for writing and literature, I chose a degree in the medical field, assuming that would help me to better understand his work. Although he seems to have forgotten, I well remember the nights I spent on-call and working overtime in a laboratory while he attended med school. When our eighteen-year marriage floundered, I found no reason to remain in the business of medicine. Thoughts of pursuing my original passion helped ease the pain my "failure" had caused. When I requested permission from the legal system to move with the children, I naively assumed any court hearing would be a mere formality. After all, I'd been assured by countless numbers of the well-meaning that custody rarely changes unless a parent becomes unfit.

The summer had proven torturous. For the first time since our separation and divorce, my ex-husband had exercised his right to extended visitation with the two younger children—they had lived with him for two months. My fear that both underwent an exertion of pressure to remain with him was realized when, on my trip to pick up the children at the conclusion of visitation, my middle daughter, the child long labeled by the family as my soul mate, refused to leave her father's house to see me. What followed I recall now as a scene surrealistic in texture, but all too real in its heartrending effect. I was actually forced to negotiate through my ex-husband and my attorney with my daughter in an attempt to convince her to talk directly with me. At last she agreed to travel with us to our new home, having secured a promise that I would not force her to begin school there until after the custody proceedings. I could see that she found the idea of losing her network of supportive peers unthinkable. Adults were no longer trustworthy, but friends were. She would tell me years later she had not chosen between parents, but between the security of her hometown and the threatening new horizon represented by Kansas City. That choice remained crucial to the custody proceedings.

As the judge returned to the courtroom to render her decision, I tightly squeezed the hand of the man I had married one month before. The hearing had not gone well. The judge refused to listen to the tape recordings of threats made against me by my ex-husband, and she didn't want to hear about the gun I discovered one evening placed upon my pillow (such accounts were declared immaterial to the question of parenthood). Nor was I allowed to speak of incidents such as the time my older daughter missed the school bus after I had already departed to my job managing my husband's medical practice. Her father was furious, because he didn't know the location of her grade school. The fact that he blamed a child for his own lack of awareness I deemed vital in predicting the quality of parenthood he would provide.

I distinctly recall the judge's punch line (appropriately named, it now occurs to me): "I do not feel the children will be able to adjust to a change in location. Therefore custody is remanded from the Defendant to the Plaintiff. Due to past communication problems between the parents, the Defendant will retain no custody. She will be allowed liberal visitation to include alternate weekends and vacations and holidays as set forth in my decision." My attorney later told me that my daughter's impassioned plea to be allowed to remain with her friends likely helped the judge make her decision. Much later I would learn that my daughter was told by her father to do what was best for her—"Your mother will be crushed, but she'll get over it."

Friends and family ventured the guess that some type of influence must have been at work over the judge; perhaps she chose to favor my ex-husband, still a resident and voter in the community, over myself, no longer a physical presence there. Or maybe she was caught up in the recent trend of breaking tradition to grant custody to the father rather than the mother. No one could accept that she had allowed a confused and panicky thirteen-year-old to determine not only her own future, but that of many family members. I wasted little time pondering the whys and wherefores; my energies were exhausted by struggling to imagine how I would survive the coming months and years without my children. The judge would later be voted out of office after a number of attorneys refused to appear before her due to her unreasonable behavior. But at that moment, I suffered not only the pain of the withdrawal of custody, but also the indignity of a lecture from this stranger regarding the paramount importance of the children in divorce situations.

❦

Immersing myself in study proved some distraction from the ache and embarrassment that was my loss. What would people in my hometown think of me, a woman whose children had been removed from her? And for what reason? Because I envisioned myself in some kind of romantic quest after literature? I returned to the classroom, struggling to absorb commentary covering Victorian humor, Romantic poets, Shakespeare's history plays. The writings of Dickens and Meredith offered little to evoke my laughter, and I obsessed over Prometheus, helpless in the face of his torture. At least I had stopped screaming at the heavens, threatening God beneath the stars over my backyard. Now I mouthed instead the ravings of medieval lunatic monarchs when I felt angry and practiced aloud the French phrases of *Henry V*'s Katherine when more placid, taking comfort in the lyrical quality of a language I did not understand. I turned past the history plays to strut and fret upon Macbeth's stage, sharing his vision of my tomorrows as evidence of yesterday's futility. And when I taught my own freshman comp classes, my voice often betrayed me, cracking around the grief lodged stubbornly in my throat.

❦

Reading Cary's lengthy history requires hours spent in the now-familiar library. Although I intend to concentrate upon the text itself, invariably I am drawn to the Reader Address. A deep and sad passion. Could this possibly be a male-authored phrase? Judith Gardiner writes of "feminist psychoanalytic insights" that, applied to the concept of female identity, "show us how female experience is transformed into female consciousness," providing us with the apparatus "with which to explain differences between writing by women and by men in . . . both form and content" (190–91). If Elizabeth Cary had written this history, why hadn't she signed her full name? I later learn such use of initials was common practice. Renaissance women rarely even published; instead, they released private copies of their works, mostly translations and writings with a religious basis, for their friends. Cary's authorship at age eighteen of a closet drama, *Mariam, the Faire Queene of Jewry,* the first, not a translation, written by an Englishwoman, was unusual. Her writing a history of an English ruler, later to be published, remains little less than remarkable. Attribution of authorship to Falkland had gone unopposed until Stauffer's 1935 claim that Cary herself had written of Edward II.

There remains today an uneasiness among critics about the history's authorship. Tina Krontiris joins the debate, analyzing what she sees as autobiographical reflection within the history, as well as a distinctive feminine approach to its telling. The work is markedly sympathetic toward the adulterous Queen Isabel, spurned in favor of Edward's male lovers, "an attitude unlikely to have been held by the ultraconservative Lord Falkland" (137).

Hungry to locate passages revealing this feminine bent, I find one early on, when the weak Prince Edward's mother is relieved of responsibility for his faults: "Neither was the degenerated Corruption in him transcendent from the womb that bare him, since all Writers agree his Mother to be one of the most pious and illustrious pieces of Female-goodness that is registered in those memorable Stories" (1–2). "Surely no male would write such a thing," I state in my seminar. Suddenly I'm known as a feminist, the very term that at first had shocked my Southern-bred, middle-aged sensibility. I embrace this new identity.

Betty Travitsky writes that "even a cursory examination" of Cary's writings reveals her interest in "the mentality and position of women. . . . Both her complete and her embryonic dramas deal with the difficulties of assertion of independent-minded women like herself" (186). Krontiris adds that Cary's emphasis on particular points of the Queen's life agree "with Lady Falkland's personal experiences as her biographers have conveyed them to us" (137). A biography?

"I've heard of it," my professor tells me in class, "but I believe it's non-scholarly and will be difficult to locate."

"I don't care," I answer the challenge. "I'll find it."

I hear another student sigh. "Armed and dangerous," he whispers to his neighbor.

After checking the *Short Title Catalogue,* I launch an electronic search. "The Lady Falkland: Her Life," the librarian reads aloud, her taps on the computer keyboard echoing her words. "Yes, here it is. Published in 1861. Looks like there are three copies in the United States." We discover that two copies are sequestered at universities, but the third is in the New Orleans Public Library.[3] A public library, I marvel.

Although neither university will release its copy through interlibrary loan, the public library comes through. Two weeks later, I hold the biography, purportedly written by one of Cary's daughters. Richard Simpson, editor of the manuscript discovered in the archives of the Department of the North in Lille, remarks in the book's preface: "The writer is clearly one of Lady Falkland's four daughters, a person of a strong and analytical mind, with much the capacity of her mother, though with none of her graces of style. The MS. was afterwards reviewed by Patrick Cary, one of Lady Falkland's younger children, who erased several passages which he considered too feminine, and added a few notes and sentences of his own; the latter I have incorporated with the text, between square brackets."

Passages he considered too feminine? I consume the text overnight, impatient of interruptions, unyielding to time or to comments made by my sympathetic husband.

"Do you have time for this," he gently probes, "with everything else?"

Everything else includes the courses within which I'm embroiled, the courses I teach, and, every other weekend, time lost, time treasured, with my children, who live three hours away. Six hours on the road minimum if I stay overnight there in my house that we've been unable to sell, twelve hours if I bring them back to Kansas City for the weekend. *Everything else* includes worries over finances; in addition to my mortgage, my husband also owns a home that sits unsold, casualty of a soft market. Dual mortgages top the rent we pay in Kansas City for our three-bedroom apartment, unnecessarily large for the two of us. We keep the oversized (and expensive) apartment for infrequent visits from the children (he has a son), who, we rationalize, need their own space. Perhaps they'll join us one day soon, after all; our hope fills the empty rooms. And my ex-husband has stopped payment of our agreed-upon divorce settlement. Missouri law states that because I have remarried, I no longer need the "maintenance" that was to represent a fair portion of proceeds from the medical practice I had managed for him for years.

"Your husband just wants to call the payments maintenance," my attorney had explained during the predivorce discussion, "so his payments will be tax-deductible. He has no intention of halting the payments in the future. This letter will protect you if you remarry." My ex-husband's attorney had written: "Her husband does not wish their financial agreements with each other to inhibit Ginger proceeding with her life if she should desire to remarry."

Upon hearing my plea, two years later, that payments be continued, the same judge who ruled in the custody case was not impressed by that plea or by my ex-husband's written confirmation of my understanding of the nature of the payments. She again supported my ex-husband's stance, because my attorney had not worded the formal agreement correctly. A week later, my ex-husband calls to say, "I was assured, by two different experts, that you would never remarry!" He calls from his new house, where my children live with his new wife, twelve years his junior, a nurse from the office I had managed. A voice in my head hums, as if singing a chorus, "Did you ever feel like a walkin' cliché?" We appeal, using a new attorney. The appeal fails.

The phone rings; it's my son. "Can you come down for my soccer game on Saturday, Mom? I'm really good this year. I know it isn't your normal day to visit, but. . . ."

Yes, I must make time for Elizabeth, even with everything else.

Cary was married at the age of fifteen to a stranger, their union representing a simple economic transaction between her father and future husband. Because Henry Cary was away fighting and imprisoned for a time, Elizabeth did not even see him for years. She lived with a demanding mother-in-law, who, finding Elizabeth unwilling to wait upon her, confined her to her chamber. She removed Elizabeth's books and commanded that no one bring her more. During this time, the young bride wrote verses. Her husband's sister conspired to bring Elizabeth writing and reading material (*The Lady Falkland*, 8–9). After seven years with no children, she had eleven in a row, nursing all except her eldest son, who was taken from her to be raised by his grandfather (11). She rode horseback for years, in spite of her being "most fearful" of the animals, because Falkland loved hunting and desired her to be an accomplished horsewoman. She "had neither the courage nor the skill to sit upon a horse." Here an asterisk appears, and I scan to the bottom of the page to read some of that material considered "too feminine" by Cary's son:

*Erased:—"and he left to desire it, after her having had a fall from her horse (leaping a hedge and ditch, being with child of her fourth child, when she was taken up for dead, though both she and her child did well), she being continually after, as long as she lived with him, either with child or giving suck." (14–15)

Later in life, her eldest daughter died in childbirth. The baby also died, but the biography notes, "had it lived, the mother was resolved to have nursed her daughter's child together with her own, not yet weaned" (25).

⟡

I think back to January 1981, when my son is born. My then-husband enters my hospital room as I lift the baby to nurse. "What are you doing?" he demands.

Surprised, I blink. The baby's fingers entwine my hair. "Feeding," I say.

"You can't," he replies, then he clears his throat, his habitual verbal signal of feigned retreat, and tries to soften his tone. "Remember? We agreed, didn't we? I need you at the office."

"But I've waited too late for the injection to keep my milk from coming in," I protest.

"Don't worry," he tells me, "it will only take a week or two for the milk to dry up."

⟡

I read in the biography that this same eldest daughter, married at thirteen, was "exceedingly beloved" by her mother-in-law and all her family. When Cary asked how she had gained their affection, the daughter replied that she didn't know "unless that she had been careful to observe as exactly as she could the rule she [Elizabeth] had given her . . . that wheresoever conscience and reason would permit her, she should prefer the will of another before her own" (13). While this statement condones wifely subjection, Lewalski says that "this apparent proposal of abject wifely submission in fact makes the wife's reason and conscience absolute judge in all cases" (184).

I am suspicious when I read a later statement attesting that Cary so respected her husband that she taught her children to

"love him better than herself," and "[w]here his interest was concerned, she seemed not able to have any consideration of her
own" (*The Lady Falkland*, 14–15). Was such dedication genuine
or forced? Was my own? I swallow hard, remembering.

❦

In 1987, after several years of rapid disintegration, my first marriage teetered upon dissolution. More and more often, my then-
husband chose to denigrate all women in general, but specifically
me, in front of our children. One evening I went up to our bedroom and discovered a handgun lying on my pillow. Because I
have always loathed weapons, I didn't touch it. I remember staring at the gun for a time, unable to form any rational thought regarding its presence. I went downstairs to ask him what it meant.

"There's only one bullet in it," he told me. "You decide who
it's for." Then he left.

Facing this decision, I seemed to have only three options, none
of which I found acceptable: (1) I could shoot him, (2) I could
allow him to shoot me, (3) I could shoot myself. Multiple choice.
I pulled the three protesting children from their beds and fled to
a motel. But within hours, I called home, fearful of his concern.
He was predictably furious over my flight. I returned with the
children, after he convinced me that my leaving was foolish, an
overreaction. "The gun wasn't even loaded," he later told a marriage therapist. "It was meant to be a metaphor."

❦

Cary's eldest daughter died in her arms as she delivered the infant
that would follow her in death. Another daughter says of Cary,
"She never gave much way to grief" (25).

❦

In February of 1981, at the age of six weeks, my infant son has been vomiting for four days. The pediatrician tells me it's flu, but the baby is happy, sleeping well. I've already nursed two daughters through several illnesses, and I know this child isn't sick; he has some physical dysfunction. I at last demand that tests be performed.

"Just goes to show, Mom is always right," the doctor tells me cheerily, following the X rays. "Our boy has pyloric stenosis. Pretty common actually—seen most often in first-born sons. The valve into the stomach won't stay closed, causing reflux of the gastric contents. With a little simple surgery, he'll be fixed right up."

"Surgery?" I force the question through a sudden fog of panic. The infant stirs in my arms; my chest constricts.

"I'm sending you to the pediatric ward now." He turns to his nurse. "Call admitting and give them the scoop. Then help Mom find where she needs to go."

I later sit behind the nurse's station, holding the sleeping baby while I cry. My then-husband finally arrives, looking very official in his surgical greens.

"Why are you crying?" he demands.

"I'm afraid," I tell him. "Patients die under anesthesia."

"Go into the conference room," he orders. "I'm a doctor, after all; I take kids into surgery every day. How can I reassure their parents when my own wife is out here blubbering?"

━━━━━━

In April of 1992, I return to the Spencer Library, copies of five scholarly articles in hand. A librarian accepts the evidence of Cary's authorship of the history.

"They argue that Elizabeth Cary is the true author," I explain. "Won't you please place a cross-reference card in the catalogue with the title of the history bearing her name?"

Lips purse. "We'll look these over," he tells me, "but it could take some time."

I smile to myself (I'm smiling more these days) as I leave the library. I guess 314 years could be considered "some time."

⟡

Cary, fluent in several languages, translated Cardinal Perron's reply to the attack on his works by King James I, but this book was burned. She later translated the cardinal's complete works "for the sakes of the scholars of Oxford and Cambridge (who do not generally understand French)" (*The Lady Falkland*, 30), although she would never be allowed within the walls of that institution. Her Epistle to the Reader states in part: "To look for glory from translation is beneath my intention. . . . I desire to have no more guessed at of me, but that I am a Catholic and a woman. . . . I will not make use of that worn out form of saying I printed it against my will, moved by the importunity of friends. I was moved to it by my belief that it might make those English that understand not French, whereof there are many, even in our universities, read Perron; and when that is done, I have my end" (*The Lady Falkland*, 172).

⟡

I sometimes dream of Elizabeth Cary, her image following even to my bed. I think of her writing her history, rejected by her husband after twenty years of marriage and eleven children, due to an act of faith. From 1626 to about 1629, Lady Falkland lived in poverty. Her husband had removed his financial support. The history was written in 1627, during which time she lived in a house without furniture, with one servant for company. She was reduced "to such want, which was in such extremity as she had not meat of any sort to put in her mouth" (*The Lady Falkland*, 32).

I dream of this Elizabeth Cary, and I wonder if she dreamed of me, if she dared to imagine a reader centuries into the future, pondering her life and writings. I choose to believe that she did. I now focus on a possible connection between Cary and Michael Drayton, a minor Renaissance poet, rumored to have been Cary's tutor. When I painstakingly compare his narrative poems concerning Edward II to Cary's history, I discover evidence to support such a connection.[4] Cary's interest in Edward II reflects that of Drayton, and the two use remarkably similar, sometimes identical, allusions and figurative language. Each time I discover a new similarity, I show it to my husband, to a wary professor I stop in the hall, to my classmates. I know now I will make the claim of Drayton's influence to help strengthen the case for Cary as author of the history.

That summer of 1992, my two younger children arrive for an eight-week visit. The first few days are strained, artificial; I will never grow used to "visiting" with my children. My eldest begins her freshman year at college in two months. She telephones, asking, "Will you ever be done with school?" Her voice echoes her father's accusatory tone. He had attended classes and training for eleven years following high school. I do not call her attention to this fact.

As I share questionable quality time with my children, I fixate on all the hours and days I've missed. The guilt I feel is relentless, but I feign happiness, swallowing the anger that I thought had abated. In the night, I weep without tears, my husband's arms close around me.

"Why," I ask, "can I not simply choose between hope and despair?"

"Life," he replies empathetically, "is seldom multiple choice."

All too soon the summer ends; the children are gone. I avoid thinking of visitation. Two weekends per month: road time is

study time lost, and each visit sharpens my pain. Too much to
read, too much to learn.

⟨✦⟩

I learn from the biography that Cary read "very exceeding much;
poetry of all kinds, ancient and modern, in several languages, all
that ever she could meet; history very universally, especially all ancient Greek and Roman historians; all chroniclers whatsoever of
her own country, and the French histories very thoroughly" (113).
The list continues, including "of most other countries something," ecclesiastical history, books "treating of moral virtue or
wisdom" (I see this passage was erased in the original), works by
St. Jerome, much of Saints Augustine and Gregory, and "of very
many others" in Spanish, Italian, or French. "Of controversy" she
had read "most that has been written": works by Luther, Calvin,
Latimer, Jewel, Sir Thomas More, and others (113–14).

I wonder over the story of her self-education. As a child when
her mother withheld light to prevent her reading at night, Cary
bribed family servants to sneak her candles, promising to pay them
when she could. By age twelve, she owed one hundred pounds.

Her marriage to Sir Henry Cary, later Lord Falkland, in 1602
promoted Elizabeth to the level of gentry, and raised Falkland,
through her fortune, from the gentry to the peerage (Lewalski,
181). Twenty years later, he "prevailed upon his wife to mortgage
her jointure properties to help raise the large sums he needed
to take up his appointment as Lord Deputy [of Ireland]" (184),
an impudence causing Elizabeth's father to disinherit her. Dated
July 5, 1627, from the State Paper Office, Ireland, a letter from
Falkland to Lord Killultagh, in the midst of Cary's isolation, reads
in part as follows:

> My very good Lord—Your letter . . . hath made choice of
> my unhappy wife for the sole subject of it. It takes notice

of a letter of hers . . . and recites several suggestions,
whereof some true and some false; the first which are true,
being only urged to induce the belief of those that are not
so, and best serve the turn she aims at; for she being re-
plete with serpentine subtlety and that conjoined with
Romish hypocrisy . . . what oblique ways will she not walk
in, hardly discoverable? (*The Lady Falkland,* 53)

Although commanded by the Privy Council to pay Elizabeth 500
pounds per year in support, Falkland ignored this command,
causing Cary to persist in her pleas for help through a barrage of
letters upon the court. In one of these, dated August 1627, she
writes to Lord Conway: "None is lother to have my Lord Deputy
discontented than I; but, alas! where the question is whether he
should be displeased or I starved, it will admit no dispute" (161).

Lewalski writes that "Falkland's harshly repressive policies
toward the Catholics in Ireland, together with his bigotry, vacil-
lation, political obtuseness, and financial folly, no doubt distressed his wife and certainly irritated the Privy Council" (184).
The king decided he'd had all he could take of Falkland, who was
called home to England in disgrace after attempting to evict all
Catholic priests from Ireland. In 1631, the Catholic queen Henrietta Maria apparently helped engineer a type of reconciliation
between Cary and Falkland, although they continued to live sepa-
rately. Cary was by his side when he died in 1633 after amputa-
tion of a gangrenous leg, caused by a fall from a horse (*The Lady
Falkland,* 49).

Ever diligent in matters of faith, the widowed Cary had her
own children "kidnaped" from their elder brother so they might
be educated as Catholics on the continent. She barely escaped
remandment to the Tower and suffered the anger of her eldest son.
In time, they reached a peace, and she lived out her life a Catholic,
an intellect, a patron of the arts. She saw six of her surviving nine
children accept Catholicism, the four daughters becoming nuns
and one son joining the priesthood. She "died . . . quietly as a

child, in 1639, being three or four- [sic] and fifty years old," and was buried in Queen Henrietta Maria's own chapel (122).

<hr />

My article regarding Cary's influence by Drayton appears in an academic journal.[5] I wish I could speak with her; I fantasize the conversation. We talk of faith, learning, literature, and their application to her life and mine, and the magic of lives intersected, though centuries apart. I tell her of my problem in locating her history, of its listing under Lord Falkland's name. She's at first amused by the idea that Henry received credit for her history. Then she sobers, her well-documented independent spirit protesting this slight. So we walk to Spencer Library, and I plead mercy from the vigilant librarians to allow her an unauthorized search of the card catalogue for her own name. She discovers a recently inserted card with the heading "Cary, Lady Elizabeth" followed by the full title of her work and the notation: E129. The card bears the date: June 1992.

Cary departs, knowing she's met that reader of whom she had dreamed, one reader in many who pursues her thoughts long after her death. And she realizes that through such study, we women of another age tend our own sharp necessities.

CHAPTER TWO

The Hystericized Woman

John laughs at me, of course, but one expects that. John is practical in the extreme. He has no patience with faith, an intense horror of superstition, and he scoffs openly at any talk of things not to be felt and seen and put down in figures. John is a physician, and perhaps—(I would not say it to a living soul, of course, but this is dead paper and a great relief to my mind)—perhaps that is one reason I do not get well faster. You see, he doesn't believe I am sick! And what can one do?

—Charlotte Perkins Gilman, "The Yellow Wall Paper"

A READILY OBSERVABLE PHENOMENON EXISTS among members of various social and/or political groups who have, we might say, little power to manage their lives in the way they want. It's called self-discrimination. I have myself seen it in action. I have myself participated in it. One may discriminate against one's self simply by giving weight to pejorative suggestions and claims made about one's group by another. Generally these claims involve the comparison of various aspects of one's self to other selves in one's culture. Gilman's story focuses on women as a group who discriminated against themselves. Although, in their hearts of hearts, they may have silently rebelled, outwardly they complied with the wishes of the men who managed their lives. Because most physicians were men, this caused a problem in women's medicine."

I listen with some distaste to my too-formal words as they drift through the large classroom, presently occupied only by me and the thirteen or so students in my Responding to Literature course. I remain mindful of a need to adjust my diction and the concepts I present to the level appropriate for the class—in this case, a general-education course. Preparing to discuss Charlotte Perkins Gilman's nineteenth-century short story "The Yellow Wall Paper," I may have already overstepped; this remains a particular weakness for me. I count on my never-bashful students to tune me in to my own overkill. Time and experience allow me some expertise in judging student reaction, and I see that these faces appear interested. I feel a certain responsibility to make my presentation *good* in my general-ed class, but not *hard*. The department uses this freshman course to tempt students into English as a major; those who find that certain affinity for literature will take their places in far more challenging courses in the future.

One student says, "I still don't get why this woman let herself be locked up."

As sometimes, but not often enough, happens, another student responds. "She didn't *let* herself be locked up. Didn't you read the story? The doctors, including her husband, just took over. What could she do? No one else even knew that she was a prisoner."

"I think she was nuts from the beginning. Look, she has everything—a vacation house, a new baby, and a husband who loves her. You make him sound like a prison guard or something."

> I don't like our room a bit. I wanted one downstairs that opened onto the piazza and had roses all over the window, and such pretty oldfashioned chintz hangings! But John would not hear of it.
> He said there was only one window and not room for two beds, and no near room for him if he took another.

> He is very careful and loving, and hardly lets me stir without special direction. (Gilman, "Yellow," 576)

A new student voice chimes in. "Yeah," it asserts, "he loves her to death."

> I get unreasonably angry with John sometimes. I'm sure I never used to be so sensitive. I think it is due to this nervous condition.
>
> But John says if I feel so I shall neglect proper self-control; so I take pains to control myself—before him at least, and that makes me very tired. . . . There comes John, and I must put this away—he hates to have me write a word. (Gilman, "Yellow," 576–77)

"Naw," someone else says, "her man didn't kill her. The woman offed *herself.*"

"Huh-uh. She couldn't really be dead at the end, because she says that she watches the dude come in and find the body."

The first voice responds. "Even if she isn't dead, like for real, her spirit is gone. It cut out a long time ago."

"I like that idea," I tell the student. "What killed her spirit?"

Comments pour forth. Her husband squelched her creativity. What did he know from creative? He was a scientist, wasn't he? It says right here in the book, it's his fault that she was sick in the first place. Oh, so having a baby is the dude's fault? No, but her depression partly is; she wasn't even sick until he convinced her that she was—that *made* her go nuts. He stuck her away from everybody and everything, and he wouldn't even let her write. That's 'cause she was supposed to be resting. Oh, yeah, she got so rested that she started talking to a lady crawling around in the wall.

> Of course I never mention it to them any more—I am too wise—but I keep watch for it all the same. There are things in that wall paper that nobody knows about but me, or ever will.

> Behind that outside pattern, the dim shapes get clearer every day. . . . And it is like a woman stooping down and creeping about behind that pattern. I don't like it a bit. It would be so hard to talk with John about my case, because he is so wise, and because he loves me so. (Gilman, "Yellow," 581)

At this point, I mention imagery typical to writing termed "feminist," because it deals with issues of importance to women— interiorities representing a woman's special place, caging or confinement, silencing by ignoring or disallowing speech and writing. I wonder aloud about the tendency for our society still to see women as representing emotion absent intellect, heart without brain. This evokes a vigorous response. Today *will* be an easy day, a day of satisfaction for me. I appreciate this class where we can discuss personal responses, as the course title suggests.

Hard concepts I reserve for my Introduction to Literary Studies class, the foundation course for English majors, minors, and teaching-certificate students. As I provide a basic intro to various schools of criticism, I simultaneously offer what, for some of the students, will serve as an introduction to the narrative elements of fiction and drama and to the myriad terms connected with the reading of poetry. We who teach the class attempt to approach it honestly. This course serves as a weed-out for certain of those whose first exposure to literature study will violate their preconceptions of the English major; we generally lose a couple of our majors here before they even begin.

My thoughts ricochet from this Responding to Lit class to the Intro class on the previous day. Same topic—different approach. In that course, I try to move beyond the "what," to examine the "why" behind this issue of the skeptical attitude of certain members of the medical profession toward complaints by their female patients and the self-doubt such an attitude evokes in those patients. I know my prejudices will interfere, but I believe that sometimes works to my advantage in a classroom scene. Students generally respond positively when my instructor's mask slips a bit to reveal the real me hiding behind a supposedly unbiased facade.

"Self-discrimination seems not to arise from any inherent force. Instead, this devaluation of self comes from outside forces. People in various disciplines have tried over time to identify the source in hopes of leading to a better understanding of self. Sociologists, for instance, speak of the human self, the manner in which one views one's being, as shaped by its culture: you are what you eat. Marxists—remember Marxist criticism?—envision this shaping as inflicted upon you, the masses, by whatever group holds economic and political power: there's no such thing as a free lunch. Those who hold to postmodern ideas, and this relates to our discussion of deconstructive criticism, feature the shaping as the result of the adherence of humans to what they call metanarratives or metadiscourse, those grand narratives, or plots, that Westerners allow to control their attitudes: the only absolutes in life are death and taxes. Metanarratives include ideas and beliefs found in religion, scientific pursuits, political ideology, any set of beliefs that claims it alone provides the Truth, the golden key to knowledge."

At last a student comments. "Yeah, so why is that a bad thing? What does it matter how we figure things out, as long as it works for us?"

"That's a big part of why you're here, in this class and others," I tell her. "You get to see other ways of looking at those 'things.' You might find a way that works better." Noticing that the fog of boredom has not yet dulled their gazes, I continue.

"Certain of these postmodern philosophers believe that words, their relationships with one another, and their symbolic meanings control our definition of reality. Words exert this control through what these same folks term *privileging*. As one might expect, this means that one idea, image, individual, etc., is better than another. Just because someone said so.

"For instance, most people educated in the Western tradition will agree that light is better than dark. We learn this not only from the Bible—I am the way, the truth, and the *light*—but from our resultant use of light as a symbol for knowledge. Not just any knowledge, but the Truth; you've all heard a phrase that incorporates the idea of seeing the light, or coming out of the dark, as discovery of the Answer."

"Like that Gloria Estefan song," a student says.

"O.K., good," I tell her, "a use in popular culture of a really old idea. Even if you never go to Sunday School, you pick up on this idea. Children, reading comic books or watching cartoons, learn that a picture of a light bulb over a character's head indicates an idea. Similarly, we learn that dark equals bad, because dark represents the opposite of light. We also learn this not only from the Bible—Satan rules a dark kingdom—but from our use of dark as symbolic for *lack*. Long representative of a lack of knowledge, darkness may be recognized only in opposition to light. A later religion, that of science, confirmed the suspicion Christianity had already posited. Where darkness exists, light remains lacking; in darkness, no electromagnetic radiation acts on your retina and optic nerve to make sight possible. What better name, then, than the Enlightenment for the period during which that new ideology or metanarrative, science, began to question a traditional ideology or metanarrative."

A lot to digest for an undergraduate class. As the students ruminate, I continue.

"Once such opposite terms assume the burden of value, they may be used endlessly as metaphors for positive-ness and negative-ness. Postmodernists and deconstructionists urge us to examine our value-laden language. Important to that examination of meaning is the examination of the source of these values. Who with what agenda has controlled our understanding of these terms/values? The understanding of the oppositional relationships of certain coupled terms remains crucial to our understanding of our selves, whether male or female. These terms that indicate sex and/or gender have long been considered opposites, and the privileging of things male over that of things female explains much of the way women relate to men in Western society." At this point, I'm interrupted by a raised hand and am immediately reminded that I teach deep within the buckle region of the Bible Belt. "Isn't that how the Bible says it's supposed to be?" I give a nod to his source, not to the validity of his privileging. I pull out my notes. "Both religion, in the narrative of Adam and Eve, and medical science in its most vestigial form as Aristotelian biology, made popular this idea. Woman is an incomplete male, a man who lacks, as Aristotle writes in *Generation of Animals:*

> Now a boy is like a woman in form, and the woman is as
> it were an impotent male, for it is through a certain inca-
> pacity that the female is female, being incapable of con-
> cocting the nutriment in its last stage into semen (qtd. in
> Jordan, 30).

"I got that information from a feminist and Renaissance critic named Constance Jordan. She explains Aristotle's ideas. The active male could contribute shape and movement to an embryo, while the passive female donated only matter. Sexual difference indicates a relationship of superior to inferior, a biological assumption that corresponds with the relationship assigned to Adam and Eve. Because the male constitutes the force that fashions the embryo from female matter, man becomes akin to God, not only superior to woman, but also divine (Jordan, 30–31). More important than any scientific value, according to Jordan, were the political implications derived from Aristotle's ideas:

> For the female's relative coldness and formlessness implied
> a whole set of characteristics that made a woman radically
> unfit for any activity that was not, in essence, a response
> to a signal or command from a man. Aristotle's politics is in

a sense an extrapolation of his understanding of biology and reflects the same preferential distinction for the soul over the body, the intellect over the passions. Because the male, exemplifying the rational element, is superior to the female, exemplifying the passionate element, it is natural, Aristotle writes in the *Politics*, that he rule and she be ruled: "this principle, of necessity, extends to all mankind." (qtd. in Jordan, 32)

I brace myself for the usual comments about women and frigidity, but they are not forthcoming. The quiet classroom, I can only hope, does not indicate a lack of interest.

"Later on," I explain, "ideas from medical science built upon statements like Aristotle's. Galen, a Greek physician-philosopher who lived and wrote in the second century A.D., takes up this idea of women as cold and men as hot, with the idea of heat being privileged. Michel Foucault, a modern philosopher, mentions Galen's ideas in his discussion of sexuality. According to Galen

> One must also take into account the heat that is particularly strong in the [body's] lower part, and singularly so on the right side because of the nearness of the liver and the large number of vessels that come from it. This dissymmetry with regard to heat explains the fact that boys are formed more frequently in the right uterus and girls in the left. (qtd. in *Care*, 108)

I remember when I sat in the same place my students occupy now, crawling along during my academic all-fours stage. Even had I heard then all of this information about why women think of themselves as second-class, I could not have effectively processed it. I returned to college for an additional degree for the very reasons feminists discuss—poor self-image, a desire for something outside the roles of wife and mother, boredom—I just didn't know it then. I wasn't even there for myself, but rather ostensibly to earn a business degree in order to manage better my then-husband's medical practice. I rediscovered my writing skills by working up case studies in business courses; when my husband later moved out of our home, a dear friend encouraged my study of English and literature, a long-neglected area of interest.

I soared through an English minor, followed by a master's degree, then stumbled a bit at the doctoral level. At first thinking I wanted to specialize in eighteenth-century literature, I made a mental sharp left turn in settling instead on seventeenth-century Renaissance study. Attracted by the idea of women attempting to write and make public those writings in a nonreceptive patriarchal society, I embraced the tools of feminist criticism to use in my study of those women and their writings. I marveled over the ideas about their lack of physical and mental capabilities that were force-fed to women "back then." One day I realized that "then" was, at least for me, "now."

I found the feminist critical method particularly satisfying and stimulating at a time when I held a dim view of the opposite sex, due to life-altering events. My gradual understanding of the historical weight behind gender discrimination aided in my ongoing interrogation of a system of justice that failed me at every turn. Recently, my interests have embraced some ideas of postmodernism and the closely related critical approach of deconstruction. Both areas of thought had initially repulsed me as spiritual wastelands, but writers like Foucault and Jean-François Lyotard offered much to my evolving understanding of discrimination and power structures through their focus on metanarrative. Lyotard I instinctively like less, as I find naturally threatening his argument that the future classroom will have no need of a professor. That reaction, however, helps me relate better to that group that represents for me the Other, my persecutors, those selves who feel their long-standing positions of economic, political, and ideological power more and more frequently under attack.

A student's voice returns me to matters at hand. "I guess what you're talking about is the need for feminism, right? I mean, I know we've studied feminist criticism and now deconstruction as tools for helping us figure out what the fun stuff means. But I'm tired of seeing these butch women on TV, talking about their rights. Like these girls trying to get into military schools. Who needs women in the military?"

"Judging from the loose zippers in the news recently, a lot of military men," a female voice retorts.

"Yeah, well, there it is. Women shouldn't be there distracting the men. They've got a job to do, and it's one women can't handle. I say, if it ain't broke, don't fix it."

"And I say you wouldn't recognize 'broke' if it sat on your face."

With some reluctance I interrupt. "Let's think about what the postmodernists tell us about why we feel the way we do about these issues. Many of our attitudes come to us through an inherited set of ideas and values, some of which may no longer apply to our society. And as for all of those bothersome women, history will tell you that changes in important social conditions will not take place in our country without the help of complaints and protests that lead to legislation."

"Down with government interference!"

I hesitate, then continue. "Think about racial discrimination. Even when people finally became enraged over the immorality of racism, only the passing of legislation made a difference in our country's actions toward minorities."

"Yeah, well, there wasn't much racism here in Oklahoma," one voice says. "We gave the black people their very own towns. Have you ever seen Langston?"

"Oh, God, girl, I can't believe you just said that."

I can. I recall similar reactions on my own part to social issues. There came a time in my life when I had reluctantly to acknowledge my own racism, not connected to any one particular event, but as a pervasive mental attitude. Although I was raised a Southerner in a segregated culture, my mother came from Illinois and my stepfather from Massachusetts. Their particular upbringing helped counterbalance the prejudice inherent to my childhood environment, so racism did not invade our everyday conversation, actions, and beliefs as it did in the case of many of those around me. I felt superior to those who used the "n" word. But I also attended an all-white school, because integration never caught up with my class. When my sister and I rode downtown on Saturday on the bus, we occupied the front seats, while "Coloreds" sat in the back. And when I sought out the water fountain in Woolworth's, I used the one clearly labeled "White."

Later, I participated in a different kind of discrimination, one against myself as a female, by my ex-husband. Many times I sat in silence listening to him expound on the inferiority of women. I feel a sickening wave of cowardice when I recall my two daughters, also forced to listen to such statements, with no intervention on my part. I also remember hearing that, like *nigger,* the word *woman* symbolized a particular mind-set, an approach to life; it was an epithet applicable to any undesirable, regardless of race or gender.

"The point is that people who want change have to get in other people's faces. It's the nature of the beast."

I remain sympathetic with my students' views. I never really understood the idea of being a member of a marginalized group until the final miserable years of my first marriage and the experience of divorce. I was shocked into numbness over the failure of the law, that most venerable of metanarratives, to protect me. Even after that life-wrenching experience, I still found myself reluctant to support feminist causes. In graduate school, I felt relief as I recognized myself in Jane Tompkins's confession of her early attitudes toward feminist criticism and its advocates:

> I wanted nothing to do with it. It was embarrassing to see women, with whom one was necessarily identified, insisting in print on the differences between men's and women's

experience, focusing obsessively on women authors,
women characters, women's issues. How pathetic, I
thought, to have to call attention to yourself in that way.
And in such bad taste. It was the worst kind of special
pleading, an admission of weakness so blatant it made me
feel ashamed. What I felt then . . . is a version of what
women who are new to feminism often feel: that if we
don't call attention to ourselves as women, but just shut up
about it and do our work, no one will notice the difference
and everything will be OK. (23–24)

The voice of my Responding to Lit student pulls me back into the
classroom to focus again on "The Yellow Wallpaper."

"I still don't understand why the lady in the story let herself
be treated like that. How come she listened to those doctors?
Couldn't she just get out of that place?"

"Like, how?" another voice challenges. "A woman couldn't
even work back then."

I nod. "That was part of the bigger problem of the way most
men, not just doctors, considered women. For one thing, a
woman was not supposed to disagree with her husband. Notice
how the narrator of the story keeps repeating that her husband
loves her, as if trying to convince herself. That was because she was
expected to comply with his wishes. Such ideas were grounded in
tradition. Even humanist writers, those supposedly interested in
physical and spiritual liberation, perpetuated these ideas. For example, here's a quotation from Rousseau's *Emile,* written in the
eighteenth century."

"The century right before the setting of this story," a student
says.

"Yes," I reply. Then I read from Rousseau's 1762 work:

On women too depend the morals, the passions, the tastes,
the pleasures, aye and the happiness of men. For this reason their education must be wholly directed to their relations with men. To give them pleasure, to be useful to them,

to win their love and esteem, to train them in their childhood, to care for them when they grow up, to give them
counsel and consolation, to make life sweet and agreeable
for them; these are the tasks of women in all times for
which they should be trained from childhood. (135)

"That guy had the right idea," the class show-off says, enjoying to the fullest the barrage of return insults from his peers.

"The fact that in this story John is a doctor, helping deal with
her illness, made things worse. Many people think science offers
all the answers, when actually, it's just one particular approach to
asking questions. There were very specific ideas about women
and their physical problems then," I explain. "Many of women's
illnesses were assumed to be related to menstruation and childbirth, and doctors often applied the label 'hysteria' to women's
physical condition."

I think of a historical tidbit I came across recently in connection with Allegheny College in Pennsylvania: "Women were
charged an extra $6.00 when first admitted to Allegheny in
1870, to cover the extra costs incurred by the 'complexity of
their nervous systems.'" At least in this instance, social reform
occurred fairly quickly: "The surcharge was soon dropped, and
a woman was senior class valedictorian by 1875" ("History of
Allegheny," 1998).

To the class, I point out the origin of the term "hysteria" as a
derivative of the Greek term for womb. "Now in the case of this
woman, she really was depressed. But what she needed was to be
able to work creatively, write, and socialize in order to recover.
The real issue is that no one could see this, especially not her
physician husband. Let's look back at the story. We consider the
narrator's voice in a couple of passages:

I always fancy I see people walking in these numerous
paths and arbors, but John has cautioned me not to give
way to fancy in the least. He says that with my imaginative

power and habit of story-making, a nervous weakness like
mine is sure to lead to all manner of excited fancies, and
that I ought to use my will and good sense to check the
tendency. So I try.

    I think sometimes if I were only well enough to write a
little it would relieve the press of ideas and rest me. . . .
There comes John's sister. Such a dear girl as she is, and so
careful of me! I must not let her find me writing. . . . I ver-
ily believe she thinks it is the writing which made me sick!
(Gilman, "Yellow," 578–79)

"That's so weird," a student remarks.

"But if you look around," I say, "you still see evidence of such
attitudes."

"John treats her like a child, or even like some kind of pet,"
another student adds. "Like she can't think for herself at all."

"Even if this story *is* based on Gilman's own experience," the
skeptic asserts, "I still say this is one incident that happened to
one woman."

"There's plenty of proof down through time of this attitude
toward women and their sanity. Many of those incidences are related to female creativity," I respond. "How many of you have
heard of John Winthrop?" A few hands inch up uncertainly. He
is identified as someone somehow connected, they think, to early
America. "An explorer?" someone ventures doubtfully.

"In a manner of speaking," I reply, "but not exactly. He
led the group of Puritans that founded the Massachusetts Bay
Colony. With him came the colonies' first published woman
poet, Anne Bradstreet. We'll have to talk about her sometime.
Her poetry was taken to London and published by her brother-
in-law, supposedly without her knowledge, or so he writes in the
book's preface. It may have been true, or it may not, but it protected Anne from the criticism of pride in having her works
appear in print. She had to concern herself with such things,
because a woman's natural modesty should prevent her calling

attention to herself. He also made clear in his preface that the writing did not detract from her housekeeping or her raising of her eight children. Supposedly, she wrote only during her hours of leisure."

Several grunts from female nontraditional students let me know that the irony of that statement has not passed unobserved.

"Some people think that her writing probably helped her preserve her sanity in the demanding conditions of the wilderness. But Winthrop, the man who helped establish the religious and civic law for Bradstreet's group, would certainly not have approved of her creative activity."

I explain that Winthrop imagined just the opposite effect of intellectual activity on females. Several of Winthrop's journal entries reflect the opinion that women suffered madness *as a direct result of* intellectual activity. In one, he notes that the wife of the governor of Hartford, a Mrs. Hopkins, had "fallen into a sad infirmity, the loss of her understanding and reason," which he attributes to her having given herself "wholly to reading and writing, and had [*sic*] written many books." Her husband later realized "his error" in allowing his wife's participation in such activities. Winthrop declares that

> had [she] attended to her household affairs, and such
> things as belong to women, and not gone out of her way
> and calling to meddle in such things as are proper for men,
> whose minds are stronger, etc., she had kept her wits, and
> might have improved them usefully and honorably in the
> place God had set her. (225)

"Yeah, but science has disproved things like that," a student says. "I mean you're talking about hundreds of years ago. That was then, and this is now."

I could tell them a story.

I think of another woman (this one's story I know well), educated of mind and independent of spirit, who fell prey to a prejudiced medical community. And why not? She simply complied with teachings of an honorable tradition, composed of various meta-narratives and submetanarratives, that represented her education both in, and outside, the classroom.

This woman, as was her habit in regard to life's discomforts, at first ignored her symptoms. They remained a matter of inconvenience and were simple to conceal. When she noticed the red splotches on her arms following a brisk walk (what exercise doesn't kill, it will cure!) she attributed them to wind burn. "Autumn is just around the corner," she told her sister later that day. "You can feel the chill in the breeze."

As she spoke, her fingers self-consciously touched the location of the splotches beneath her discreet long-sleeved blouse. That night she checked her arms before going to bed with her husband. Only the freckles she had hated since childhood peered back at her. Pragmatic to a fault (my German blood, she told her children), she decided to dismiss the incident. Surely she had imagined those blotches.

Peering in the mirror days later, she noted the strange bright pink discoloration of her nose. She blew hard into her handkerchief, once again regretting the weeping nose and stuffy head that accompanied any weather change. But she'd lived with it all her life, this "darn runny nose." She smiled at that nose in the mirror, musing, Thank goodness I didn't meet the neighbors on my walk. They might have thought I'd been drinking. And at this hour of the day, too!

Another month passed; she had stopped taking her constitutional in the cold morning air. When her husband, a sedentary man who admired her energy, asked about it, she explained, "I've been too busy." On the day the pains began, she experienced a twinge of fear. She recalled as a child telling her mother of aches in various places. "Remember, big girls don't whine," her mother would say. "It's probably all in your head anyway." She must have been right, because the aches always disappeared. Later, before her first husband had been killed, he teased about her infrequent complaints, saying, "That's the meanness coming out in you." The fleeting memory made the woman smile as she thought of him, forever boyishly handsome. How long ago had that been? Forty years now?

She learned to distract herself with household duties during the brief durations of pain. Although she didn't feel like cleaning the house, her ancestry reminded her, "Work is good for body and soul. Cleanliness is next to Godliness." When, after more time passed and she could no longer stand the physical work during her attacks, she turned to intellectual pursuits. Reading had long been a passion, and she could always write to the children; both activities served to pull her attention from the pain.

She had such fine children; all had made her proud. And they could keep a decent correspondence, too. The round robin letter had been her idea. Knowing how children could drift from their families, and how the demands of marriage and parenthood could make writing a problem, she had started a circulating letter. The rules were simple. She had explained them to all involved, including her sister, who also contributed. Read all of the letters in the packet. Remove your old letter, put in a new one, and send it on to the next family member in the prearranged sequence.

How she looked forward to that round robin. Such a nice, fat envelope containing at least five letters, and sometimes drawings from the grandchildren. She always watched for its bulk passing from the mailman's hand to her own about six weeks after sending it away. It became even more important now.

The splotches, sometimes accompanied by a raised rash, came with greater frequency, in reaction to any change in temperature. The pain had settled in her lower stomach. A newer symptom appeared, that of ravaging hot flashes. How embarrassing to explain to her husband. Shouldn't such things have disappeared long ago with her loss of the ability to have children? His concern was real. "You should see a doctor," he told her. She told him she probably would, if "it" got worse. When the next round robin came, she wondered, "Should I tell the children?" She remembered the angry reaction of her middle daughter when she'd once been in the hospital and had not told any of them.

"I didn't want you to worry," she said.

Her daughter's response had startled her. "Don't ever do that to me again! I want to worry. Please grant me that privilege."

She would never have talked to her own mother that way, but her daughter's words made her feel somehow proud. Still, it was silly. Maybe she would tell them later, if it got worse. Her iron will stood her in good stead in the past; surely it would serve her now.

A schooled woman, she had traveled; she knew something of the world. For a period she taught school herself, then quit to marry her first husband. Back then, a married woman couldn't teach school. After he died, she worked part-time in a physician's office in exchange for medical care for her three young children. Later, after remarriage and the birth of her fourth child, she taught again—English, Latin, and French. Because she faced such chaos in her early adulthood, she now craved order. Her children knew well the force behind her orderly household.

One day she told her husband, "I've got to go to the doctor, but don't worry. I'm sure it will be something simple." It wasn't.

To the doctors' credit, they at first listened carefully to the woman's complaints. Always one who demanded accuracy from others, she required no less of herself, and she described her affliction in detail. They performed every test available. The tests reflected no results to account for her symptoms of increasingly painful lower abdominal discomfort, splotching of the skin when exposed to a temperature change, and hot flashes that set off crippling waves of nausea. She was treated with dyspeptics, told to rest, to lie down with the onset of pain, to eat carefully, to drink lots of water.

"They don't know what's happening," she finally explained to her children. "But it's getting worse."

Her children, living away from home, didn't know what to think. Their mother was a capable woman; surely she could find help. The older ones solicited the opinion of their youngest sister, a nurse, and the sibling closest to home. Like the woman, the sister could only trust in the doctors' expertise.

Now the round robins contained her guarded statements of hope for future testing. Months passed. The pains increased, not only in intensity but in duration. At first she hid her despair and frustration, but both began to mount.

"I've been poked and prodded to death," she wrote. "I must have had every test known to man. No one can tell me anything. They just keep asking me to describe my symptoms. Sometimes I think the doctors hope I'll change my complaints to something they know how to handle. And the bills keep coming."

"I'm afraid," she told her middle daughter, "that they've stopped listening to me."

"*Make* them listen," her equally frustrated daughter said. "Make them." The distracted daughter could not imagine anyone ignoring the forceful woman under whose demanding supervision she had matured. Her mother would surely work this out.

***

My in-depth early grounding in science allows me some knowledge of the patronizing attitudes of medicine toward women, and, in a lesser degree, all patients, regardless of gender. I married into a family composed in part of four male physicians and two registered nurses. My immediate family boasted, in addition to me as a medical technologist, one registered nurse and two biochemists. This family texture allowed perpetual insight into the world of science, one admittedly filled with promise, and an obvious sympathy for its admirable aims. But after graduating from training to participate within the medical community and the world it serves, I noticed that something strange had occurred in popular culture's view of science. It had been elevated to the status of religion, with physicians acting as post-Enlightenment priests. Now, light years removed from my early career, I find postmodern philosophy's ideas regarding metanarratives particularly applicable to the stranglehold that science and medicine enjoy over those caught up in certain Western traditions.

In few cultures do physicians enjoy the esteem approaching near-deity status granted them in the United States. Even while a physician's wife, dedicated to perpetuating the myth of medicine for the good of the public, I believed that a tendency to confuse technical skill with power over life and death had caused society's substitution of the physician for God. This dangerous exchange remained grounded on the misperception that doctors possess metaphysical capabilities beyond the scope of the normal human. Unfortunately, many established medical practitioners help perpetuate this confusion, a fact evident through the material value they place on their limited technical skills. When one professes to sell health and longevity, price becomes moot to one's customer. Medicine seeks to control its own market, all the while disallowing the participation or input of the consumer in the practice of its pursuit.

The medical students I knew twenty-five years ago and with whom I shared a few classes, while not yet touched by greed and power lust, understood to some degree the wealth and power their futures promised. Even though I observed those students treated like scum in medical boot camp by their superiors, they still managed a fledgling feeling of superiority over their patients. They had to; it was part of the drill. "You're the doctor, for God's sake," they were told, as if they automatically acquired mystical powers by slipping their arms into a white lab coat.

In discussing the manner by which a postmodern philosophical approach helps to understand the metanarrative labeled science, Robin Usher and Richard Edwards evaluate its practice by examining ideas of T. S. Kuhn. Kuhn writes that the scientist is formed by, and acts through, "an unconscious acceptance of traditional, community-based authority, an authority which provides a way of theorizing or understanding, working on and changing the world" (qtd. in Usher and Edwards, 37). Yet the scientist tends to reject the very culture that grants science its authority. I had observed this myself in the form of a condescension toward the great unwashed among the physicians with whom I had contact.

Ideas of Usher and Edwards may explain the kind of "denial" physicians seem to suffer when considering their relationship with, and dependence upon, members of society whom they should embrace as patients needful of their skills, yet whom they seem to regard instead as customers seeking a commodity. Any social centering of science admits the possibility of its existence only in relation to something else. It admits the presence of an "other" in the form of an irrational community presenting a constant danger to the desire of science for total control. Science seeks to "know" in a manner independent of history and culture. It desires a "common standard" allowing the reduction of difference to sameness, heterogeneity to homogeneity. Without this "elimination of difference," science cannot declare the mastery that is equated with knowledge, and it loses its privileged "authorising center." This causes science to be "both lacking and without lack, masterful yet always seeking mastery." The concept of "lack" works here as "the sense of incompleteness, uncertainty . . . another form of otherness; a failure to master is always present and without the aim of completeness, certainty and mastery would be impossible" (37–38).

Such attempt at mastery is not without cost. Physicians as a group retain the dubious honor of having the highest incidence of suicide and chemical and alcohol addiction among those calling themselves professionals. Many of those forced to work and/or live with physicians describe them as controlling, strung out, always wired while in public. My experience with the day-to-day functioning of various medical practices revealed that the physician often delegates responsibility, but not authority; thus, most medical offices suffer an incredibly high turnover of employees. Most of those employees are women—underlings. The defense of the offensive behavior often demonstrated in relations with/to co-workers and subordinates (family members may be seen in this light as well) remains the worst type of convoluted logic: physicians may behave in any manner they please, because they are physicians. They know the path to Truth. In many circles, this attitude has been labeled with great disaffection the "god complex."

Foucault's notion of the "discourse of knowledge, power and truth" encompasses scientific pursuits. He proposes that once a certain means of discovering truth is promised through a metanarrative, such as science and its subset medicine, any competing ideas that don't satisfy that metanarrative's preestablished conditions are rejected as false, ideological, based on belief/intuition. Thus, as Usher and Edwards write, other ways of knowing

> are suppressed or debased, e.g. religious truth based on revelation, notions of Platonic truth based on Ancient Greek conceptions of truth . . . the knowledge and truth of literature. . . . They are suppressed, ignored or marginalised because they do not have the status of truth. It is hardly surprising, therefore, that Foucault refers to powerful discourses as "regimes of truth," giving as examples medicine, psychiatry and other forms of disciplinary knowledge. In describing them in this way he alerts us to the *politics* of discourses. (85–86)

When a patient appears with a set of symptoms, physicians attempt to match those symptoms to some previously recorded observation through consultation with medical histories in journals or manuals, the handbooks of their regime. These books resemble those used by any technician who consults predetermined parameters. My personal observation of the methods by which physicians interview their patients reveals their tendency to guide the patient's replies in a manner that fits the predetermined pattern of disease as presented in the medical literature. The occasional patient whose responses vary from the rules vexes the physician, who may feel challenged, even threatened, when his metanarrative cannot supply a ready answer. In this approach to action, the practice of Western medicine highly resembles the practice of Western law. Law is not about justice; it is about following the recorded letter of the law (hermeneutics). Both of these practices have inherited a set of rules (a metanarrative) that claims to provide the pathway to Truth. Even though they are self-limiting, metanarratives, such as that of science, refuse any admission of limit. To do so would be to accept that rationality has a measured usefulness, "that there is a different, nonrational, incommensurable knowledge which science cannot know" (Usher and Edwards, 38). Like any generality, the one I present above will not fit all cases or all physicians. But for those patients whose trusted doctor refuses to believe their statements, often with tragic results, statistics do not impress.

A grave problem in the pursuit of medicine is the lack of an adequate definition of the term *life* beyond its relationship to death. Practitioners of the body cannot point to the locus from which life emanates, although that has been attempted by ostensibly pinpointing responsible organs. Early ideas attributed the life force to the liver, then to the spleen. Later, the heart received credit, and more recently the brain's activity, electronically measurable under certain circumstances, was granted this weighty honor. But that is not the complete story. Anyone who has ever viewed a human death realizes that much more than electronic impulses forms the force that departs the body when life ends.

That life actually remains an unknowable quantity causes us to attribute to it a mystical quality. Ironically, in spite of science's efforts to debunk the metaphysical, spiritual/religious/ superstitious impulses still capture the human imagination, which links this practice of intuition to the practice of medicine. We go so far as to say that doctors hold power over life and death in their hands. The Western esteem of these combined metanarratives basically grants physicians license to do as they will, because the Western mind has confused the practical with the spiritual.

If this were not enough ground for confusion, that much-revered metanarrative that declares the superiority of the male body and mind over those of the female cannot help affecting the practice of medicine. Ongoing scientific studies continually disprove theories regarding the capabilities of functions of females, yet the religion of science,

> by passing itself off as objective, dispassionate, disinterested and universal in its applications . . . has disguised how partial and distorted its construction of knowledge is. Through being associated with "nature," women are part of the otherness which science both seeks to master and thinks it has mastered. (Usher and Edwards, 38)

Foucault comments that the definition of "sex" in the nineteenth century especially was built on the idea that "there exists something other than bodies, organs, somatic localizations, functions, anatomo-physiological systems, sensations, and pleasures; something else and something more, with intrinsic properties and laws of its own." This method of interrogation of "sex" contributed to the process of the "hysterization of women." One definition of sex was "that which by itself constitutes woman's body, ordering it wholly in terms of the functions of reproduction and keeping it in constant agitations through the effects of that very function." Within this vision, "Hysteria was interpreted . . . as the movement of sex insofar as it was the 'one' and the 'other,' whole and part, principle and lack" (*History*, 152–53).

❦

Before many more months passed, the woman experienced agony much of the time. Her pain and hot flashes were unbearable, yet they had to be borne. One day while making an emergency visit to her physician, she lay on the examination table, her husband fanning her furiously in an attempt to provide the slightest relief from an internal heat so intense that she feared it might consume her body. When the doctor entered the exam room, he could not conceal his exasperation over her repeat appearance. He pronounced her mind as the source of her misery; she suffered from "hysteria" due to a mental imbalance. Tests proved there was nothing physically amiss; therefore, he suggested admission to a psychiatric hospital ward.

The suggestion devastated her. As a person who craved order, she found the thought that she could not control her own mind repulsive. But enveloped by pain with no explainable cause, she began to doubt herself. "Maybe it *is* all in my head," she told her middle daughter tearfully. "I'm so embarrassed."

She lay in the psychiatric ward for several days. As her discomfort grew, something she thought impossible, ward rules prevented her eating. A member of the staff ordered her to retrieve her own tray from the meal cart parked in the hallway. "It's an important part of your therapy. If you don't serve yourself, you go hungry." Because she could no longer leave her bed without considerable hardship, she did indeed go hungry. Before long even the desire for food departed in the face of unremitting pain.

A member of the staff ordered her to attend the ward's group-counseling session. "It's an important part of your therapy." When she explained that her allergy to the ever-present cigarette smoke in the group meetings would make her sicker than she already was, her "complaint" was duly noted. As were her "complaints" about pain. As these complaints increased, so did the quantity and dosage of her sedatives. When her middle daughter called, she sounded confused and disoriented. Over the next forty-eight hours her mumblings quickly dissolved into incoherency.

Within a day, the youngest daughter contacted her older sister, sobbing uncontrollably. "Mother has liver cancer," she finally managed to say. "She's in surgery with a ten percent chance of survival."

This is what had happened. The woman drifted into a coma over a matter of hours. When a nurse discovered her with an abdomen that "made this sixty-four-year-old woman look nine months pregnant," she became alarmed. When the woman began vomiting feces, the nurse decided to act. She did not call the woman's psychiatrist of record, but instead summoned a surgeon. He took one look at the comatose patient and ordered her into surgery.

The surgical procedure revealed a twisted gangrenous intestine, obstructed by a tumor. Several feet of intestine had to be removed. The woman had a rare form of cancer, known as carcinoid. The youngest daughter searched her medical books for a description. She discovered that a carcinoid is a slow-growing tumor, accompanied by symptoms of skin splotching and hot flashes. The woman's case was textbook perfect, but little observed.

The year was 1984.

The woman was my mother; I was that incredulous middle daughter. My reaction to the events at the time remained complicated by the presence of so many medical people within my family circle. It was further complicated by the fact that, although never consulted in the case, a brother-in-law was actually part of the group medical practice that misdiagnosed my mother's "complaints." I heard a number of times, and perhaps for the first time, "Doctors aren't perfect. They make mistakes." I also heard from one indignant sister-in-law who was not a scientist or physician but a doctor's wife, "If she'd been a man, they'd never have put her in the psych ward."

❧

"Do you think stories like 'The Yellow Wallpaper' ever really make a difference? I mean, do they change things?"

Another student reminds us that in Gilman's explanation of her reasons for writing the story that follows it in our anthology, she notes that she sent a copy of "The Yellow Wallpaper" to her specialist, a real-life physician referred to by Gilman's narrator. He never acknowledged having received it. Gilman writes that the story "has, to my knowledge, saved one woman from a similar fate—so terrifying her family that they let her out into normal activity and she recovered" (589). Then she adds that the "best result is this. Many years later I was told that the great specialist had admitted to friends of his that he had altered his treatment of neurasthenia since reading 'The Yellow Wallpaper'" (*Why*, 590).

"So he was one of the good guys," a student adds, "not afraid to admit he was wrong."

"Right," I said. "He showed courage, too, by rethinking a bit of that metanarrative."

As the students depart, I look back to a chilling passage from the story's first few paragraphs: "If a physician of high standing, and one's own husband, assures friends and relatives that there is really nothing the matter with one but temporary nervous depression—a slight hysterical tendency—what is one to do?"

What, indeed?

I think of my mother's miraculous recovery only days short of her sixty-fifth birthday. After bucking overwhelming odds to survive the surgery itself, she faced a life-span prognosis, if aided by chemotherapy, of five years. "That's all right," she told me, "I never wanted to live past seventy anyway." She would succumb to the carcinoid two weeks short of her seventy-seventh birthday.

I don't think Mom believed in miracles; she'd rather trust herself to accomplish what was needed. Although her life would be forever altered, she had been given a chance at survival. That chance was all that she ever asked from the medical community. Her will did the rest. Years later, one of her friends was examined by the surgeon who performed Mother's emergency operation. The friend told him that my mother still credited him for saving her life. No one was more tickled than Mom when she heard of the surgeon's stunned reaction: "You mean that woman is still alive?"

She told me that as she dressed to leave the hospital, her nurse suggested she visit her medical specialist at home. Just point to that surgical scar, the nurse urged, and say, "This is the latest cure for depression." Although my mother would never do such a thing, her physician had to have heard of the incident.

I still wonder, did he become one of the good guys?

CHAPTER THREE

Writing the Light Fantastic

Come, and trip it as ye go
On the light fantastic toe,
And in thy right hand lead with thee,
The Mountain Nymph, sweet Liberty. . . .

—John Milton, "L'Allegro"

HAVING WANDERED A LARGELY misdirected path into my late thirties before deciding that a return to the reading/study of literature would best serve my desires, intellectual and otherwise, I suffered years without the comfort of my early love of books. As a young reader, I had longed for books to transport me from my gray existence into one of melancholy blues, passionate reds, envious greens, elated yellows, even desperate blacks. I entered into an unspoken contract with authors I tested; I offered them my reading-heart to break. I dared writers to crack it, rend it and leave it craving more as I reluctantly closed books, wishing for that never-ending story. Emancipation, "sweet Liberty," from life's burdens accompanied reading, and my imagination rose on its own light toe. I applied my reading-mind, of course, approaching books with a willingness to accept intellectual gifts. But it was the hunger of my reading heart I sought to satisfy.

I return now to that intimate relationship with reading, the effects of every weary step I took to get here likely etched on my

mid-age countenance. But this time, I want to be on the other side
of the reading contract to which I have so often willingly agreed.
I seek not for my own heart to be broken, but to break the hearts,
those trusting reading-hearts, of others.

I don't want merely to touch readers. A jolt, a rude intrusion
into their comfortable reality, an experience—Milton's trip, at
once light *and* fantastic, I long to provide. My big discovery is
that I want to share. But that desire erects a barrier to my role as
academic. For in my critical writing, I am asked most often to
project a personality described by Frances Murphy Zauhar as
"authoritative" and "objective" (105) without focus on myself as
a reader or on the personal effects of my reading. An authoritative voice lacks the promise of indulgence, play, or liberation that
I seek to offer.

A different but related personal conflict with the professional
study of literature exists for me in academe's seeming reluctance
to share its discoveries/realizations with the popular reading public. Many academics, otherwise seemingly starved for audiences,
recoil at the idea of writing for those readers who eagerly desire
to trip from gray into a more colored existence through reading.
Because I have already published a number of stories and articles
for popular audiences, I find the negative attitude on the part of
my academic peers toward popular publishing both disconcert-
ing and confusing.

Well into graduate studies, definitely having arrived at that
point from which I could not turn back, I began to receive strong
signals from those-in-the-know that my writing suffered from
certain deficiencies. Intuitive and emotional aspects of my writing were summarily dismissed as nonprofessional and, even more
insulting at my stage in life, immature. My intellect remained
equal to the challenge, the authorities assured me, but my writing
style required major alteration. The desire to share my enthusiasm for another's written work in addition to offering analysis
and professional reflection caused my intellectual mask to slip,

inviting personal intrusion into the attempted application of the so-called objective scientific method. Look for the Truth, they said, the assigned articles I read said, the *PMLA* said: make it *impersonal*. I felt rather like a patient, expected to rejoice over a positive prognosis that depended on surgery to remove an offending limb.

In considering their advice, I was blinded by a glare of contradiction. They asked me to omit elements of self, to cause my ideas to hit the page reflecting no aspects of the struggle it took to get them there. Yet one can identify meaning in the work of another only through relation to self. When reading, most people search for characters with whom they may identify. The search may be unconscious or excruciatingly self-conscious, but it proceeds. The self tells us, "I am like her," because in that empathy lies acceptance and understanding of a character's motive. Such a method applies to the reading of nonfiction as well, but reader empathy aligns with the words and ideas of the unseen author along with her or his topic. Again, motive remains all-important to reader acceptance. Humans know humans; all the words in the world cannot mask a bogus sincerity.

Yet I was being told to write without sincerity, without offering the reader an empathy point, without supplying any of my feelings, and this I found a challenge, not to mention a cause for consternation. As a useful tool in honing one type of writing skill, it certainly has its place. But I reject this dry, impersonal, unimpassioned presentation as the lone measure of my skill as a scholar. This idea of the perfected seamless work I think of, basically, as a bit of a fake. It's more like offering the reader a *seems*-less work; seems less personal, seems separate from the author's private life, seems less than it could be. An intimation, a secret shared, any bit of the personal, where appropriate, can in many instances offer balance to the reader immersed in heavy academic research. She may benefit from the reorientation afforded through personal commentary on matters that, presented as objective narrative, may appear unrelated, and unrelatable, to her life experience.

Many esteemed scholars offered up to fledgling academic writers as exemplars divorce both feeling and instinct from their intellect. In this divorce, a certain importance of their words falls away, because the reader cannot learn why the information presented remains important. The information provided may lead to a better understanding, a knowing, of an issue, but where is the value in understanding without application to self? We read everywhere that literature focuses on the human condition, so how can criticism of that literature ignore the purpose for which its subject matter exists? As Olivia Frey says, "reading and writing are interactive processes that involve the whole self, so that feelings will influence thoughts" (53).

Apparently part of the rejection of a more intuitive approach to writing involves the association of that approach with things feminine, and thus somehow lacking, by a largely male group of scholars. G. Douglas Atkins asserts that "this model of literary professionalism, which effectively converted the critical—certainly the evaluative or judgmental—into the scholarly, was designed to remove the aura of effeminacy clinging to the study of literature" (46). His discussion of the founding of the Modern Language Association in 1883 and the journals that soon followed gives some insight into the historical rejection of the critic who was also a poet, and, apparently, a womanly poet at that. Some scholarly journals making their appearance at the close of the nineteenth century "established the (masculine) article as the form—almost immediately the only form—acceptable." After mastery of the journal article, one might graduate to composing the monograph, "understood as a longer, better, more virile and potent version of the article." Sadder still, English programs became "dedicated to the production of research scholars," using this form of writing "to instill and promote rigor" (46). The one inkling of hope in this historical presentation may be found in Atkins's phrase that "*not much* has changed since those heady, formative years" (46, emphasis added). He indicates that some change, however small it might be, has taken place. That small degree of change offers promise through the rebirth of personal criticism.

We are hardly surprised to learn that feminist criticism plays no small part in the rejection of the scientific approach to academic writing as the only legitimate technique. Olivia Frey declares that

> To put it bluntly, if it were not for women, we might not be questioning the way that we write literary criticism. If women had not been suppressed and denigrated in the particular ways that they have, and responded to their pain as they have by forming a sort of feminine subculture, we would not have new values with which to compare the conventional values of our society and our profession. (60)

Atkins suggests "the possibility of a *familiar (essay) estranged*— a reorientation of the essay in English" culminating in a personal criticism like that found in feminist theory. A theory of this sort "provides both hope for and one direction toward the achievement of such a possibility. Such a possibility, at the moment frankly experimental and groping for a form, would not separate the professional and the personal, the autobiographical and the critical" (14). I shared this hope long before I could give it a name. That we might touch the reading-heart as well as encourage a knowing-heart seems a noble goal.

Nancy Miller defines personal criticism as entailing "explicitly autobiographical performance within the act of criticism," explaining that such writing "typically involves a deliberate move toward self-figuration, although the degree and form of self-disclosure of course vary widely" (1). This personal criticism, containing "self-narrative" within argument, raises what Miller calls "crucial questions" concerning not only "the constitution of critical authority" but also "the production of theory" (2). That

this method involves confession and perhaps a bit of megaloma-
nia and even masochism no one will argue. But any type of writing intended for publication cannot be divorced from the writer's
ego; even if published anonymously, the writer still receives a private delight at seeing her words in print that she would miss if the
writing never left her desk. One could go so far as to argue that
any voluntary act of committing words to paper involves the ego
in its desire for expression beyond the thought process.

While Atkins's statements and those of other male scholars
act to contradict the idea that the desire for autobiographical criticism remains peculiarly feminine, this approach definitely appeals
to feminist writers. These writers, like Frey, join with others in
seeking "a new language that is accessible, concrete, real, an embodiment of the feminine" (41). According to cultural edict, such
embodiment may be deemed inappropriate to those critical-writing
conventions long accepted as standard in academe—lacking in
soundness, too dependent on narrative, too contextual. Writing
that falls outside conventional objective discourse may be rejected
as too experimental.

When first navigating these troubling waters, I neither believed nor desired that a single approach should be adopted for literary criticism. I longed—and my opinion on these matters has
since further strengthened—only for the acceptance of personal
criticism as legitimate, meaning acceptable for publication and for
doctoral dissertation work. That some journals welcome personal
criticism—and we may hope for additional venues soon to appear—remains a relief for those who depend on publication for
the retention of professional positions and for the receipt of tenure
and/or additional promises of economic and professional security.

Feminist critics, among others, continue to propagate through
example the ideas of writers such as Henry James who expressed
the importance of personal impression in reflection about literature. In the essay's long history, it appealed to a popular reading
public who depended on such personal reflection for under-

standing. Atkins writes, "No matter how theoretically sophisti-cated or analytically acute we become, we cannot avoid, nor should we minimize, impressions and personal response; literary experience stems from the former and is arid and insignificant without the latter" (48). That public readership dependent on this personal expression should remain privy to discoveries of, elucidations of, and reactions to literature. A return to writing for the popular public promises a boon to academics who scramble to find audiences and venues for publication.

Literature acted on me exactly as intended. It offered me not only a manner for reflection—but also for self-reflection and growth. Not to be able to write of the import of this occurrence during graduate school, during the very time at which the effect was strongest, seemed the cruelest and most illogical of prohibi-tions. There had to be room somewhere, I recall thinking at the time, for something in addition to the scientific, objective critical article, a more personalized criticism. Even a self-indulgent writer, after all, might represent a myriad of other selves who could carry something useful away from the blend of the personal with the critical. Some of those other selves might even exist outside the academic arena. Do not those who study humanities, at least those supported by public funds, have a responsibility to make some small part of the knowledge that results from their research accessible to the public? This seemed an impossibility when I pe-rused articles requiring a collection of research aids to glean un-derstanding from overelaborate diction and inflated tropisms.

One day, as I considered the impersonal approach commonly employed by scholars of academic writing, and how one might defend the inclusion of the personal, I thought about the use of dedications. The dedications appearing in the opening pages of many books aimed at academic audiences do add a small touch of the personal to any discussion that follows, a fact noted by Jane Gallop, among others (1149–1150). This matter of dedications in general recently assumed great importance to me in connection with one particular dedication made by Elizabeth Cary of the closet play that she wrote during her teen years. We find a venerable history supporting the act of dedication in a volume titled *Index of Dedications and Commendatory Verses in English Books before 1641*. Not only does the collection contain dedications, but it also includes records of intended dedications that for various reasons did not see print or were recalled. A message appears beneath the section headed Canceled Dedications, alerting readers to the fact that "Dedications canceled before or just after publication sometimes escape destruction." Entry 4613 reads "Carew, Elizabeth. The tragedie of Mariam, 1613. H.D. HN. Mrs. Elizabeth Carye [see Greg, 308]." As discussed in Chapter 1, in my early studies of Cary, I had encountered the various interchangeable spellings of her surname—Cary, Carye, Carew—and remained privy to the confusion caused by the lack of traditional spelling in Renaissance writing. Adding to the confusion that makes for a challenge in researching this period is the existence of multiple Elizabeths possessing a surname of Cary/Carey/Carew.

Scholars guess that Cary canceled the dedication to the person ostensibly serving as her dear friend, identified as either her husband's sister or his sister-in-law. The cancellation may have resulted from confusion caused by both the author and dedicatee possessing the same name. Because that dedication remained on many copies of her drama, this confusion led to some question of Cary's authorship years later, a confusion that was cleared up, in part, by the notice of John Davies's dedication of his "The Muses Sacrifice" to Cary; he refers to her play set in Palestine. This fact in itself confirms the vital importance of the dedicatory address.

While many writers fashioned Renaissance dedications in the hope that the dedicatee would become a patron and contribute to the writer's support, Cary did not have that idea in mind. Her dedication hints at a most important relationship, stating of her sister-in-law that, after her absent husband,

You are my next belov'd, my second friend,
For when my Phoebus' absence makes it night,
Wilst to th'antipodes his beams do bend,
From you, my Phoebe, shines my second light.

Many points of interest intersect here, including Cary's demonstration of her knowledge of the accepted trope of the male as sun, the female as his reflector, or moon. Also important for its glimpse into her personal life, the dedication establishes Cary as one with a connection, an inspiration, and a comfort drawn from the presence of an other.

This long-accepted manner of addressing the personal seems at least to open the academic door to considerations of including additional personal reaction and information in scholarly writing. Those who question the validity of a personalized criticism would not contest that dedications personalize writing, nor could they suggest that the revelation of this personal voice in any way detracts from the theory that follows. The dedication exists as part of what Diane Freedman realizes when she writes "that every book, every reading, is laced and surrounded with circumstances worth considering, border crossings within the text as well as its edges" (Freedman, Frey, Zauhar, 3–4). Surely I am not the only one who cannot read a dedication without immediately conceptualizing its author as a human being. Generally the dedications suggest, if they do not blatantly state, a relationship on the part of the author with other beings of flesh and blood, separate and apart from the topics their writings discuss. Names of parents, lovers, children, friends, and instructors grace countless books; indeed, they introduce the books, literally acting as a foundation for the bound paper we hold in our hands, while having provided a groundwork in life for the author. The dedicatory phrases may or may not relate to the book's content, but they relate directly to the writers. They alert readers that one's existence does not consist of a perfectly formed fabric, free of stitch and seam.

One would expect to witness personal addresses to important others in works by authors who permit within their text a glimpse of their personal selves. In Richard Rorty's *Contingency, Irony, and Solidarity* (1989), notable for its description and discussion of the "ironic liberal," the dedication reads "In memory of six liberals: my parents and grandparents," and Janice Radway dedicates *Reading the Romance: Women, Patriarchy, and Popular Literature* (1984) simply "For Scott." Miller's *Getting Personal: Feminist Occasions and Other Autobiographical Acts* (1991) is inscribed "In Memoriam LK," and Atkins states in his preface to *Estranging the Familiar: Toward a Revitalized Critical Writing* (1992) that his first book was dedicated to his parents, and "it is only fitting and right that I dedicate this one to them as well: with love and prayers and thanks." As editors of a 1975 collection of articles discussing language and its relationship to sex, Barrie Thorne and Nancy Henley dedicate their work, *Language and Sex: Difference and Dominance* (1975) "To our mothers, Alison Cornish Thorne and Estella Ziegenhein Main, in sisterhood." Scholarly people do not write in a void, any more than they live in a void, and these names and relationships make impossible the acceptance of scholars as nameless experts.

But what of those authors who adopt a more traditional and objective approach to research and criticism? I pull additional volumes from my shelf, perusing just those at hand. I open Weller and Ferguson's 1994 edition of Elizabeth Cary's *The Tragedy of Mariam,* and read on an otherwise blank page, "To our mothers, Mollie Weller and Mary Anne Ferguson." Aubrey Williams dedicates *Poetry and Prose of Alexander Pope* (1969) "To Michael, Christopher, Katharine, Mary Margaret, Rachel, and Donald." Katherine Usher Henderson and Barbara F. McManus in *Half Humankind: Contexts and Texts of the Controversy about Women in England, 1540–1640* open their volume with "To Ellen, Matthew, Geoffrey, and Tracy Henderson and Ginger and Jack McManus." *John Milton: Complete Poems and Major*

Prose (1957), edited by Merritt Y. Hughes, bears the words "for Jane and David, Elspeth and John."

Thomas Roche, I learn on the first page of a 1978 edition of Spenser's *Fairie Queene,* possesses an impressive mini-vita, and one completely matchable by mini-vitas at the front of a myriad of scholarly books. At the time of publication, he served as an English professor at Princeton, having been educated at Yale, Cambridge, and Princeton, and he had written and edited several additional works, including ones focusing on Shakespeare, Petrarch, Ariosto, and Tasso. What gives Professor Roche a face is not this list of professional accomplishments, but rather the conclusion to his Note. Here he offers his gratitude to his wife with the hope that he does not, through his list of duties with which she assisted him, diminish "her real and unacknowledged contribution to this edition." The most traditional of critics, perhaps some who question the wisdom of the personal comment in conjunction with the scholarly, have themselves already shared a glimpse into their lives through dedications. Such words allow readers a brief glance at a personal dimension of those who otherwise may remain fairly anonymous.

These dedicatory phrases compose in part the contextual framework of the text itself. The very few words of the dedication remain blatant reminders that those scholars who may, as Peter Carlton confesses once to have done, aspire through criticism to "objectivity, validity and inclusiveness" in an attempt to "master and control the literary text" (240) needed personal relationships long before attempting mastery and control. Carlton later joined ranks with others in rejecting the repressive objective approach in favor of personal criticism. The importance of the exhibition of control over our topic fades, the concept itself becoming unnecessary. Instead, we offer our readers the opportunity to identify with our own involvement with authors and characters, their ideas and dreams. In this involvement our fabric connects to that of others, not only our contemporaries, but also individuals from another age. Rachel Blau DuPlessis writes that she challenges "the sustaining fiction of objectivity, distance and neutrality in critical studies; a writer has to need what s/he writes, and to need it in ways that implicate other people" (viii). Perhaps those who question personal criticism believe that the autobiographical elements work against the writer's credibility as a scholar, that the personal should be silenced when one approaches literary criticism. The legitimacy of such a claim obviously may be countered.

As I continue to reflect on the traditional (meaning linear, logical, authoritative, unchanging) approach to the study of literature, I incorporate into that consideration my recent interest in the philosophy of postmodernism. I find particularly intriguing its connections with feminism and the importance to the criticism of literature of any intersection that might appear in the agendas of these two fields of inquiry. Postmodern thought remains valuable to some types of feminism in a consideration of the historically subordinate position of women as real—not an abstract, but instead a concrete concern with which women deal every day. Some postmodern thought pulls the rug of esteem from beneath metanarratives of Truth; the Authorities, particularly Patriarchy, involved in a search for that Truth; and Knowledge built on gender assumptions. One problem in this intersection, however, is the postmodernist's passive approach to concerns of women, such as marginalization, upon which feminism wishes to act. Postmodern thought is just that—passive ideas, not a blueprint for action. But even though postmodern philosophy seems at first to neglect the importance of agency to feminists, a close examination of the practices it allows reveals the existence of political potential. That potential is found in approaches to writing like that of personal criticism.

Agency may be discovered in a postmodern approach to narrative in which aspects of the private may be brought to bear upon the public. History and all official versions of truth may be reenvisioned, because personal criticism focuses, as does a post-modern agent, on the act of questioning and seeking, on examination of a multitude of possibilities that may substitute for the traditional version of the answer. The inclusion of personal reflection in nonfiction writing allows us to avoid that singular trap perpetuated by our constant seeking after the Truth, the trap into which we are lured by our taught desire to locate Truth. Every declaration of Truth, or so it seems, has eventually been debunked, making liars of those who promise its existence. Personal reflection allows us the escape from that trap, a method of musing that substitutes legitimately for declaration.

<hr />

Naturally I understood in graduate school the necessity of sharing the results of my research on Renaissance English playwright and historian Elizabeth Cary in formal writing; of examining Meredith's *The Egoist* through written criticism for a class on Victorian humor; of agonizing over my paper (the rough draft bore my professor's note, "a distressing number of to-be verbs"), "Man as Metaphor in Shakespeare's *King Henry IV, Part I*," for a seminar on Shakespeare's history plays; of recording the results of my investigation of sources for the writings of Anne Bradstreet; and of identifying and discussing in a conference paper feminist elements in Dashiell Hammett's novella *Woman in the Dark*. My struggle to produce terse research prose reaped some benefit; I celebrated, as did my professors, the fact that papers based on three of these endeavors subsequently saw publication in traditional refereed journals. At least a portion of the frustration I felt over having to exclude any aspects of personal intuition or emotion from my academic writing found release in my writing for a popular market, where such an approach remains not only acceptable but encouraged. Many of those same professors who celebrated my success in academic publishing did not, however,

seem to value the concurrent publication of my stories and articles in *Highlights, Turtle, Write Now!* or *The Single Parent.*

As for myself, I couldn't really judge which of my publications
I valued the most. Each represented a victory in terms of my life
process; each provided evidence that I could shape a future while
finally claiming the promise of my past. Early reactions of certain
professors when they learned of my popular publishing, however,
worked to devalue that aspect of my writing career. Although
friends outside academia suggested that those within eschew writing that reaps financial rewards, I found that explanation lacking.
I could not explain their negative view of my outside writing activities in any satisfactory way. But I took seriously certain signals
on the part of the authorities that convinced me not to share news
of further publications. Thus, my progress through graduate
school carried with it a silencing effect, in that I found life simpler
if I kept my publishing for a popular audience to myself. This
problem, coupled with my repressed desire to write with feeling
about my studies, created much dissonance for me as a writer.

Of course it was bound to happen; the day arrived when I desired to share with that approved reading audience not just information about Elizabeth Cary's closet play and her history but
what the study process had meant to, and done for, me, as an individual. Simply expressed, it had a transformative effect on my
vision of self, and I felt this was vital information to share. Such
an approach would not be tolerated in my seminar on early Renaissance women writers, or in any of my other courses on the
Renaissance.

I at last discovered an outlet in the seminar on the personal essay conducted by Professor Atkins. Doubting the rumors I had
heard about the freedom given to students to include the personal
in the papers required for this course, I entered the classroom
on the first day to learn that it was true. Along with my fellow
students, whose large numbers filled the small seminar room to
bursting, I might indeed indulge in personal commentary in liter-

ary criticism. At last I had discovered a venue for the discussion, not merely of Cary's works and milieu, but of my growth as a person due to the study of those works. Parallels between Cary's life and my own nurtured my feminist criticism of her writings. Many nights I drifted into sleep thinking of the woman, the person separate and apart from her writings, and awakened with the same topic on my mind. While Cary's play, history, and translations offer tremendous appeal as topics worthy of attention, her position as a woman, and our positions as women trying to live conscientious lives in the midst of an oppressive society, offer actual spiritual sustenance. The resultant paper subsequently appeared in one of the few journals open to personal criticism and later competed for a feminist writing award.

That experience, as far as I can tell, inflicted no damage on my intellectual approach to basic research that leads to literary criticism. While I continue to wince under the infliction of the "have to's" of traditional research writing, I participate in this requirement more willingly, knowing of the additional outlet afforded by personal criticism.

A few years following my seminar, in the midst of dissertation work, an opportunity arose for me to write a biography for young adults, those popular readers, about Elizabeth Cary. That biography acted, to my knowledge, as the first book with Cary as its subject aimed at a popular reading audience. I did not share much information about the book project, or my joy in its composition, with my professors, although it represented what I considered a noteworthy result of traditional research. I felt they might disapprove of the fact that I spent energies on the book that I might have devoted to my dissertation. I also feared a negative attitude toward my writing for that audience, an attitude that could prove a political detriment in the future. But I feared even more shirking the great responsibility I bore to liberate this woman. I desired to free Elizabeth Cary from a silence inflicted on her not only in the sixteenth and seventeenth centuries but in the twentieth century as well by the confinement to academia of information regarding her existence.

What accounts for my desire? I remain irresistibly attracted to Elizabeth Cary, to the Cary that existed apart from, yet integrally as a part of, those concerns important to traditional research: her proper employment of Senecan elements in her drama, her proper applications of contemporary instructions for correspondence in her letter writing, her proper use of sources for her history. Here are some of the things about Cary that attract me—no, that connect me—to her. In the Argument prefacing *The Tragedy of Mariam, Faire Queene of Jewry,* Cary describes Herod's desire to exclusive possession of Mariam, a desire so strong that he orders her murder in the event of his own death, as "dangerous affection." I know of such affection that remains dangerous unto death, and we all observe it daily in shameful statistics concerning spousal abuse. I recognize as autobiographical reflection on the part of Cary the fact that the villainous Herod in one scene takes to bed with a headache in order to "sleep away my woe" (4.7.524). Cary herself did so throughout her own life, often from headaches accompanied by an overwhelming melancholia, the source of which was nothing in general but everything in particular. I know that ache and that melancholy, of working through a haze of pain that nauseates and exhausts by turns. In the same play, the chorus tells us regarding the innocent Mariam's beheading by her irrationally jealous husband, "'Tis not enough for one that is a wife / To keep her spotless from an act of ill: / But from suspicion she should free her life / and bare herself of power as well as will" (3.3.215–18). These words grew from Cary's own experience in seventeenth-century England, an experience motivating her to present to her daughter upon her marriage a ring inscribed with the cryptic phrase "Be and Seem." She knew the importance of seeming to the world, an importance I recognize as well, where I sit writing in the midst of an early-twenty-first-century culture yet unforgiving of the imperfect female.

That Cary produced England's first closet play written by a woman, was wife of a Deputy Minister to Ireland, mother to eleven, and may have written a history of Edward II bearing only the initials "E.F." to indicate authorship, remains important. Equally important to me is that she wrote that play while remanded to her room by an irate mother-in-law with pirated materials sneaked into her by her new sister-in-law; that Lucius, her first child, was removed from her care to be raised by her own parents, who had no son; that that same son would take her place in inheriting her parents' fortune when they disowned her for her husband's act; that for a time she would be known to history only as mother to Lucius; that her ambitious husband practiced misogyny, referring to Elizabeth as a snake in correspondence; that the history "possibly" written by Cary would have been produced during her persecution for conversion to Catholicism and remained the product of, according to its author's note, "A deep and sad passion" (Weller and Ferguson, 16). These circumstances join not only our intellects but our sensibilities, shared passions seaming our lives together in a near perfect match.

Apparently as a young girl, Cary surprised everyone when she mastered the art of the seam. As with languages, she could not be taught needlework; she had to learn it on her own. Because sewing remained so vital a skill to women of her era, not only for reasons of providing domestic comfort but also as a mark of the lady, her shocked family apparently felt great relief when they saw her wield the needle as skillfully as the pen. Her biographer tells us that "she was skillful and curious in working [needlework], but never having been helped by anybody; those that knew her would never have believed she knew how to hold a needle unless they had seen it" (*The Lady Falkland*, 186).

When I first read this anecdote, I remembered my own failure to produce a decent-looking garment in my eighth-grade home economics class. I did not understand even the mechanics of sewing on a button, much less those of putting together a dress. I still recall my sharing aloud in the middle of class with my best friend the consternation I felt at not understanding why the thread would hold when one passed the needle through the button's eyes. "You embarrass me," she said softly, ducking her head in an attempt to avoid the gazes turned our way. My consternation dissolved into shame at the simplicity of her explanation: "You tie a knot in the end of the thread before you pull it through." I detested sewing and proved it by scoring in home ec the lowest grade I ever made in any class. One day my instructor pointed at the dark circles under her eyes as she returned to me a simple shift I had basically destroyed in its construction. "You're the reason for these bags," she told me. "I worried all night, because I had to give you a grade of 'D.'"

My thoughts fast-forward to high school when, lacking the resources to purchase much in the way of new clothes and tiring of my sister's hand-me-downs, I decided to teach myself to sew. Suddenly I mastered the threading of the machine that so confounded me before. I watched with admiration the clean, sure movement of the needle dipping its head beneath material, searching for bobbin thread loop and resurfacing, having locked into place one in an inviolate chain of cotton links capable of bearing incredible strain. I loved choosing a pattern designed by someone else, then finding my own perfect material to fit that vision; I loved the clean cleaving by the scissors of the carefully pinned pattern pieces from a stretch of material; I loved watching garments take shape from strange looking pieces of fabric that fit together like a jigsaw puzzle, joined by seam after seam.

I continued my handwork for many years, crocheting throws and knitting comforters as gifts during those first student-poor years of marriage, later moving on to elaborate cross-stitched and embroidered creations, sewing the requisite matching outfits for my two daughters, dabbling in quilting by making a cover for my eldest child's bed to match her curtains. Those creations now seem a lifetime away, a part of another woman, as indeed they are. On a recent visit to my younger sister's house, I came face to face with a crocheted throw, circa the mid-70s, and it startled me through time. An artifact of another age, it awakened memories, not all pleasant. I lifted the throw for close inspection and spotted a dropped stitch here, a lumping knot there, symbols of the uneven landscape of my life—imperfections that are me.

Now I seam my creations on a computer screen, the clack of the spinning sewing machine wheel replaced by that of quickly depressed then released keys, my material only the words in my mind. The long-revered connection between sewing and literature I intimately understand as I work just as hard to seam paragraphs together as I did material, yarn, and thread. I think of Atkins's comment that, "Applied to essays, the metaphor of piece work as quilting points up just how dependent these things are on quotation, cut from the full cloth of other text(ile)s" (20). My writing will never represent the perfect seamless product, any more than did my sewing, a fact in which I take pride, for those seams, knots, and dropped stitches reveal my connections to life. Homer's Penelope also connected, weaving by day, ripping by night, a cycle of creation and destruction moving her forward through time. Charles Dickens's Madame Defarge connected, knitting revolution into her scarf, the stitches foreign to a proper pattern, shaping a story with pattern of its own. Susan Glaspell's Mrs. Hale knew the power of the slipped stitch, recognizing in poor handwork an admission of guilt by a wife who strangled her husband, connecting to him her hate with knot neat and clean. Adrienne Rich's Aunt Jennifer found in her tigers a creative escape from the manacled connection of her wedding band. Imperfect lives stitched and woven, proud of their seams, knots, and dropped stitches.

Personal connections made in academic writing promote a new layer of connection with the reading-heart, as well as with the reading-mind. The objective, seamless presentation may remain admirable, but at times one wishes not to admire, but rather to acquire, assimilating another's story as one's own. This works on multiple levels, allowing a reader to identify with an author and with the author's subject, as the author's own identity with subject matter becomes clear in the reading. If the goal of academic writing remains one of understanding on the part of the reader, why not encourage such assimilation, rather than prohibit it? Intuition and imagination lead to knowing as surely as does intellect.

The writing of my stories produces other stories, and the following I relate to audiences at writing conferences. My Cary biography began as a twelve-page proposal for a collection of chapter-length biographies focusing on early women writers. My suggestions for subjects included Christine de Pizan; Queen Elizabeth I; Mary Sidney, Countess of Pembroke; Elizabeth Cary; Anne Bradstreet; Margaret Cavendish, Duchess of Newcastle; Katherine Philips; Phyllis Wheatley; Mary Wollstonecraft; Harriet Beecher Stowe; the Brontë sisters; Emily Dickinson; and Virginia Woolf, among others. I submitted the proposal to fifteen publishers. All but one returned encouraging letters, what I term positive rejections, praising my idea, but explaining the reasons why they declined the project. About a year after I first developed it, the proposal, along with two sample chapters, one on Elizabeth Cary and one on Margaret Cavendish, made its way to a new publisher in response to a call for manuscripts that appeared in a writing newsletter. A month later, I finally received the phone call about which I had fantasized.

When the publisher identified himself, I took a deep breath and prepared to focus on his comments and questions, assuming he would identify those women he wanted to include in the collection. Instead, he asked immediately, "Would you be interested in writing a book-length bio just on Elizabeth Cary?" Needless to say, his remark elicited surprise, followed quickly by pure joy. When I asked the publisher, also his fledgling company's sole editor, what made him choose Cary, he told me, "The sample chapters led me to believe that, of the two women, you have a greater emotional investment in Cary." The suggestion stunned me, for I could detect no difference between the two chapters. As one writer friend stated, "What a perceptive editor! You must work with him." I did.

My first experience with the publication of a book-length work did not lack challenges. The fact that I worked with a non-academic editor presented its own set of demands. Along with the normal amount of editing that exasperates any author, the galleys reflected alteration or blurring of certain facts for the sake of audience interest that simply could not be allowed. But those problems remained solvable. Later, amusement more than irritation struck me with one reviewer's comment that, while more books about women from this period were needed, Cary lacked enough name recognition to merit a book. I thought the book was needed for that very reason! My disappointment over one "bitchy" (my publisher's choice of descriptors) review that pointed out as a weakness my not explaining why Cary chose conversion to Catholicism I tempered with the realization that this comment came from that same popular audience, untrained in research, for whom I had specifically chosen to write. That individual either did not realize or thought unimportant the fact that we have inherited no historical evidence to support a discussion of Cary's motivations. I could not simply fabricate information for the sake of a good read. My disappointment was further tempered by the announcement several months after its publication of the biography's inclusion in the New York Public Library's catalogue of recommended reading for teens. When I received a copy of the catalogue, the note attached directed me to the page number on which my entry appeared, and bore the comment, "We look forward to your next book." Naturally, I found this gratifying for purely egotistical reasons, but also as a clear indication of a need for such a sharing with the public.

In the meantime, I continued submitting my proposal for a collection of chapter-length biographies on several women; too many positive comments on the idea had been made for me to cease seeking a publisher. When I received an envelope from a press that I recognized as the publisher of various books used during my research over the years, I assumed it contained yet another rejection. So great was my surprise on discovering a two-page letter from the publisher that I almost dropped the sheets of paper. The voice behind this letter rang confident and competent, commenting upon my suggestions in an informed manner. In responding to the section of my proposal focusing on Elizabeth I, the editor mused that Elizabeth chose her words carefully

> not so much because she was a woman but because she
> was an astute politician and could take the tenor of the
> times and turn it to her advantage. By protesting the weakness of her sex she could successfully pull off a number of
> strong-arm tactics before her opposition could react. This
> is quite different from pussyfooting around because she
> was a female, and I would wager that women through the
> centuries have used the same sort of legerdemain in the
> kitchen as well as on the throne.[1]

I obviously shared much in common with this publisher, and we pursued our correspondence over several months.

When I mentioned the reviewer's comment regarding Cary's not being worthy of a biography, the publisher wrote back, "that's a reviewer trying to sell books, it would seem to me, which is not a reviewer's job. . . . I agree with you; it begs the question." Later she told me, "I am not an academic but my husband was (18th-century English literature) and my interests as an editor tend to be a little on the scholarly side. This is not always the best thing in the current marketplace, but I believe in presenting kids with things that Ms. Viola Swamp of the local high school doesn't even know about." My enthusiasm toward this kindred spirit grew, as did our joint vision of the book.

I continued research to find women meeting her criteria for subjects. The publisher embraced my suggestion to include Delarivière Manley (1663–1724), author of libelous fictions and a favorite of fashionable society. She wrote, "Of the women you mention, it seems to me that Manley is good because it gives a different view of what a woman with a pen could do. I suspect most kids think that Queen Victoria is the paragon of femininity for several centuries (kids aren't so good on dates) and a sort of Erica Jong type would be excellent." What she told me next, I heartily endorsed:

> I am thinking now that what this book could be about is women as writers; different kinds of writers—rather than just as good writers, or worthy writers. This gives you the chance to show them as women, in their selves and various social roles, and relieves you of the burden of having to prove them "good" writers. . . . [P]erhaps it's enough to say that they affected the society in which they lived, or their writings tell us a lot about women of their times, or that they were women of either great courage, intelligence, privilege, or stamina.

The book would feature Christine de Pizan (1365–1430?); Teresa of Avila (1515–1582); Elizabeth Cary, Viscountess Falkland (1585–1639); Margaret Cavendish, Duchess of Newcastle (1623–1674); Katherine Philips, the Matchless Orinda (1632–1664); Aphra Behn, the Incomparable Astrea (1640–1689); Gluckel of Hameln (1646–1724); and Delarivière Manley (1663–1724). In a refreshing statement, the founding publisher, who also served as acquisitions editor, urged me not to read into the women writers "what you want your thesis to be," adding, "I am not in any political camp as an editor: I just want our books to be true to their subjects and not propaganda."

Being true to our subjects—this may exist as our ultimate challenge as writers, whether for the academic or popular market. The omission of political agenda in factual writing naturally remains a necessity, while its inclusion in other approaches might be welcomed. Writing at many levels for multiple audiences offers demands that may arouse in some a near-schizophrenic state. But for those who enjoy multiple audiences, whether based on age, gender, or subject matter, both the formal and the personal approach to multiple genres and avenues should be available for the exercise of this writing. Whether or not a writer accepts the postmodern premise that all approaches to knowing and the discovery of truth remain equally important, tolerance toward that attitude should be encouraged, particularly within academia, which ideally serves to encourage investigation and experiment as well as the imitation of traditional forms. One must, as Virginia Woolf desired, keep "the flight of the mind, yet be exact" (324).

My writing remains, at times, a frustrating endeavor. Still I struggle, feeling now and then that old and welcome challenge to stretch, to be sharp and dangerously aware. I focus on Milton's words, attempting to capture in my own the seeming contradiction of the light fantastic and the freedom it affords; to this I aspire. Although treading lightly, I determine to leave behind footprints worthy of measure. I stalk my prey as I have been stalked, searching for willing victims, for others who want to fill their reading-hearts as well as their minds.

CHAPTER FOUR

Putting the Flowers In

The courage that my mother had
Went with her, and is with her still:
Rock from New England quarried;
Now granite in a granite hill.

The golden brooch my mother wore
She left behind for me to wear;
I have no thing I treasure more:
Yet, it is something I could spare.

Oh, if instead she'd left to me
The thing she took into the grave!—
That courage like a rock, which she
Has no more need of, and I have.

—Edna St. Vincent Millay,
[The courage that my mother had]

A S A CONSUMER AND TEACHER of literature, I urge my students to probe writings by others for elements they might apply to their own lives. The recognition of one's self in another's work remains my single most important hope for students in my introductory literature classes. Sometimes I see that recognition in their eyes, and on rare occasions they share the sense of identity with me. One student told me that on a first attempt, she could not finish reading an assigned poem because the poet described her family perfectly: "It was like she was sitting on my front porch, looking in our windows."

Like most other teachers of literature, I discuss some works again and again in introductory classes. Some of them appear as familiar as an oft-traversed path; one easily recalls the landmark characters and plot, the metaphor and rhythm. But this familiarity may suffer a jolt when we encounter new experiences in the interim since last communing with a work. Suddenly the piece demands renewed focus and concentration as we undergo identification of, and appreciation for, certain elements not previously noted. Such a phenomenon took place for me following the loss of my mother.

My mother's death on June 14, 1996, forever altered certain of my most fundamental approaches to living. I have had by necessity to reformulate the manner by which I perceive myself and my relationship to others. For months following her death, items and activities I formerly prioritized in a neat mental list quickly dissolved. Now that list was comprised of a single item— acceptance. This acceptance, requiring a conscious act of will on my part, included not only an acceptance of her physical disappearance, but also of my new position in life as one lacking parents, without the psychological and geographic roots of my youth.

This struggle is nothing new, in a universal sense, but it remains painfully new to me. Although I had ample time to prepare, I discovered that nothing can adequately cushion one against the ensuing tidal wave of sorrow that follows death. Still, knowing that innumerable others have ascended from this abyss, I search for help from their experiences, and I find some aid in the same literature I've read for years.

Writing and reading are both helpful approaches to handling many types of loss, whether of innocence, independence, security, love or another human being. Our own written contemplation may function as a cathartic activity, while reading the writing of others may serve vicariously to help us reach understanding. In my attempts to acknowledge and accept, I consider both approaches and turn first to reading. I think of one of my favorite periods for literature, that of the seventeenth-century Renaissance. In England during this more formal era, written guides offered instructions outlining the "correct" way to approach the work of acknowledging the loss of a life and celebrating its memory, commonly called an elegy.

Most published elegies from this era are written by men, but not all. Anne Bradstreet, writing in a New World, but definitely a part of the English Renaissance writing tradition, was one of the women who turned to writing elegies to ease her own grief. Interestingly enough, one popular guide to various types of writing, *The Arte of English Poesie* (1589), referred to simply as "Puttenham's," was labeled by Edward Arber, nineteenth-century editor, a "Ladies book" (3). The author of the instruction book writes that he appeals to a narrow feminine and/or courtly audience, the book's chief purpose being "for the learning of Ladies and young Gentlewomen or idle Courtiers, desirous to become skilful in their owne mother tongue, and for their private recreation to make now and then ditties of pleasure . . . specially for your Ladies and pretie mistresses in Court, for whose learning I write" (6). Bradstreet may have consulted Puttenham's, or a similar manual, in commemorating the deaths of various family members.

The elegy finds its place as "The forme of Poeticall lamentations." Puttenham's notes that although lamenting remains "contrary to rejoicing," one finds "a peece of joy" in being able to lament "with ease, and freely to poure forth a mans inward sorrows and the greefs wherewith his minde is surcharged" (61). This form remains appropriate to the consideration of "death and burials, of th' adversities by warres, and of true love lost or ill bestowed" (63). I like knowing that centuries ago writers acknowledged the healing effects of their craft. The term *lament* I prefer to *grieve;* it seems, for reasons I can't clearly explain, a

more active approach to dealing with sorrow. The poet confronts
the sorrow that might otherwise seethe within, producing distraction and debilitation.

I review Bradstreet's elegies, noting ways in which they conform to rules of the day. As she praises her parents, she adopts a
formal tone and structure, using proper pronouns and employing
rhyming couplets. Had it not been for Bradstreet's "An Epitaph
to my Dear and Ever-Honoured Mother Mrs. Dorothy Dudley,
Who Deceased December 27, 1643, and of her Age, 61," history
would know nothing of an obviously courageous and determined
woman who braved a wilderness and helped her family thrive.
Bradstreet describes her as "A worthy matron of unspotted life, /
A loving mother and obedient wife, / A friendly neighbor, pitiful
to poor, / Whom oft she fed and clothed with her store," and is
careful to insert a reference to her mother's piety and faith, clos-
ing with mention of her children and grandchildren. Bradstreet
eased her own grief as she celebrated a life that might have otherwise gone unnoticed. I consider again the importance of writing to our handling of loss. We don't know whether the death of
Mrs. Dudley caught her daughter by surprise, but we can tell that
Bradstreet misses the obvious role model her mother represents.
Bradstreet craved that courage that her mother took to the grave,
a craving that Millay would share centuries later, and I a few
decades after Millay.

Bradstreet worked within a patriarchal tradition, and she
carefully complied with the male model of writing that she inherited. This becomes especially apparent in the elegiac "To Her
Father with Some Verses," inserted posthumously into the second
edition of her *The Tenth Muse* (1678). She expresses appreciation
for her celebrated relationship with a father who encouraged her
early reading and study and who later held various civic offices
in the Massachusetts colony, including governor. As Bradstreet
praises her father's accomplishments, she also emphasizes her
feelings of eternal debt. That idea of debt to a parent I relate to

well. It's the kind of debt one repays only by passing along the love and consideration received from a previous generation to the generation that follows one's own.

Bradstreet, then, repays that debt to Mr. Dudley with words meant to be read, not by him, but by generations to follow. This act represents one in many that Bradstreet can undertake to pass along her heritage. It also allows her to leave something of herself behind for those who will one day grieve her loss. Renaissance poetry often celebrated the earthly immortality available to a subject through verse. The simultaneous immortalization of the poet as a creator is something the majority of writers in any age crave. What could be more seductive than the promise of escaping through words the obliteration caused by death, or of helping a loved one do the same? Bradstreet was not innocent of this ploy, and when she writes that, if her work reflects any value, "Who can of right better demand the same / Than may your worthy self from whom it came," she not only celebrates her father as worthy, but also as her muse and inspiration. She lightens her sorrow through the profession of belief that her father's spirit will survive in her written words. As a writer, she employed her craft in remembrance of another. Her words achieved the same quality of permanence that those on Dudley's gravestone achieved. In a manner of speaking, then, the writer can cheat death.

We tend to feel guilty for our anger over death; at least I do. After all, we know from childhood that it will come, so wouldn't a mature person accept and move on? Doesn't my reaction to my mother's death indicate some type of weakness? I wonder if that weakness grows from my not being a particularly religious person, in the formal sense of that term. A close look at Bradstreet's reactions supplies further material for my musings. History tells us that Anne Bradstreet seems to have served as a near-perfect model of Puritan piety. But grief seldom promotes perfection in actions, regardless of one's strong constitution, and some of her elegies reveal a slipping of that pious mask. This slipping offers me comfort, and I willingly accept the possibility that my own silent protest against the injustice of my mother's tortured death may color my reading of Bradstreet's response. I find that response in some of her elegies, works that clearly depart from a silent acceptance of God's plan for her and her family; she *does* question the justice of the deaths of younger family members. Wendy Martin writes that Bradstreet's work "constitutes a female counter-poetic" (ix) to the patriarchal idea of "providential destiny" (15). Providence translated to God, the founder of the patriarchal system of Puritan behavior with which Bradstreet usually complied. Usually, but not always. Of secondary interest is a hint of Bradstreet's own feelings of guilt projected through some of her elegies. Her guilt derives from the fact of her longevity, in comparison to the short duration of the lives she mourns. The obvious irrationality of these various survival guilts, mine and hers, whatever their cause, makes that guilt no less difficult to bear.

For Bradstreet, like the rest of us, destiny may have seemed to be in the hands of a sometimes unfeeling Providence, one that cares little for human grief. Examination of her poetry reveals a personal struggle with the temptation to rebel against Providence's cruel and inexplicable whims. Her writing affirms her experience, according to Martin, "in a society that . . . often denied women a voice" (6). Bradstreet's elegies reflect this affirmation as she gives voice in writing to her struggle to accept the deaths of those removed from her in an untimely fashion. The complaints she registers to the metaphysical power believed responsible for both the giving and taking of life I find comforting in my own state of emotional dissent.

Bradstreet's "reverence for life," and deep sorrow at the interruption of such life by death, remains a theme of much of this poetry. As Martin notes, Bradstreet's theme of "generativity . . . radically challenges patriarchal ideology and politics" (6) that embraced the survival of the fittest as its own and as God's law.

Cases in point are the elegies Bradstreet wrote in memory of lost grandchildren and of Mercy Bradstreet, wife of her eldest son, Samuel. In a poem written to Elizabeth Bradstreet, who died at the age of eighteen months, the poet begins by chastising herself. She knows she should not bewail the child's fate, since it now lives in eternity. Another type of guilt surfaces. But her tone undergoes a change in the second stanza. She voices a protest against the removal of one so young, an act that goes against the laws of nature governing the life that Bradstreet observes all around her:

> By nature trees do rot when they are grown,
> And plums and apples throughly [sic] ripe do fall,
> And corn and grass are in their season mown,
> And time brings down what is both strong and tall.
> But plants new set to be eradicate,
> And buds new blown to have so short a date,
> Is by His hand alone that guides nature and fate.
>
> —(In memory of my dear grandchild
> Elizabeth Bradstreet, etc. 2.1–7)

Bradstreet's grief finds some relief in protest against the unnatural aspects of the child's death. I am reminded of my mother's departure, one far removed from the ideal of a naturally peaceful death that occurs during one's sleep. My own spirit rises to protest the unnatural suffering, the acute anxiety my mother had to endure before her release was gained.

My favorite Bradstreet elegy marks the memory of another grandchild, who died at three years and seven months. A reasonable tone is noticeably absent here. In this poem, Bradstreet unleashes a lamentation that reveals to the reader the strength of the tie she felt to little Anne Bradstreet. She suffers in spite of any patriarchal idea that death is to be accepted:

> With troubled heart and trembling hand I write,
> The heavens have changed to sorrow my delight.

> How oft with disappointment have I met,
> When I on fading things my hopes have set?
> Experience might 'fore [sic] this have made me wise,
> To value things according to their price:
> Was ever stable joy yet found below?
> Or perfect bliss without mixture of woe.
>
> —(In memory of my dear
> grandchild Anne Bradstreet, etc. 1–8)

Her unanswered questions ring as a demand for understanding from a silent universe. Try as she may, Bradstreet cannot hide her rebellion against death's unmerciful acts. Most interesting to me is the poem's focus on its speaker, which greatly exceeds the energy spent on the dead child. This, after all, is the truth of death, and one I only now realize: those left behind cannot escape the strong effect of loss and the normal reaction of anger that often follows.

Bradstreet frames her greatest anguish in an elegy dedicated to Mercy Bradstreet, a woman she clearly loved. She projects pain for herself and also for Samuel, whom she addresses in her elegy through apostrophe. Not only did Samuel lose Mercy, but he lost four of their five children (Martin, 92). The weariness of the survivor rings in her tone, and I wonder if she ever also longed for death, a longing with which I can, in small part, identify. I recognize that tone as present in the comments of my mother just prior to her own demise. Of her multiple losses, Bradstreet writes in part:

To the memory of my dear Daughter in Law, Mrs. Mercy Bradstreet, etc.

> And live I still to see relations gone,
> And yet survive to sound this wailing tone;
> Ah, woe is me, to write thy funeral song,
> Who might in reason yet have lived long,
> I saw the branches lopped the tree now fall [sic],
> I stood so nigh, it crushed me down withal;

My bruised heart lies sobbing at the root,
That thou, dear son, hath lost both tree and fruit: (1–8)

A babe she left before she soared above,
The fifth and last pledge of her dying love,
Ere nature would, it hither did arrive,
No wonder it no longer did survive.
So with her children four, she's now at rest,
All freed from grief (I trust) among the blest;
She one hath left, a joy to thee and me,
The heavens vouchsafe she may so ever be. (21–28)

Bradstreet suggests in her first lines a question many of us ask, and one I know that my mother asked—why do I live while so many others die? Discovering my mother's written comments relating to this topic following her death helps me, I suppose because we didn't talk about her impending death as much as I think we might have. I've wondered whether it would have helped her to talk more about it. I discovered a Christmas card letter she wrote to friends in December 1992 that assures me she had no trouble speaking of death. However, she had as much trouble accepting losses as anyone else: "I had a horrible time for a while. Within five months I lost my husband, two brothers, a dearly-loved sister-in-law, and five friends. Then there were mishaps while some repairs and changes were made in my house, the worst being that the first contractor *died* in the middle of it." I look back at Bradstreet's poem, in which she clearly believes that Mercy's death flies in the face of reason; she will not be comforted. Her later parenthetical comment, "(I trust)," gives me pause. She seems to waver when counting on the dead's release from suffering, and who can blame her? All these centuries later, we still lack proof of an existence after life. Bradstreet's words, and my mother's own, portray an insecurity that I find comforting in my own present insecure state.

My quest for acceptance left no part of my life untouched. Even my outlook on the most familiar stories altered. As I now envisioned those works through the lens of my loss, my teaching was affected. One day, while reviewing Katherine Anne Porter's "The Jilting of Granny Weatherall," I mentally staggered beneath the sudden weight of a nauseating sorrow. Scenes so familiar that I could practically recite them from memory assumed a newly symbolic significance that left me astounded. Images with which I had previously interacted easily now bypassed my mind's eye to lodge uncomfortably in my heart. I did not think I could deal with such private pain in the public forum of the classroom. In the figure of Cornelia, caring for her dying mother, I suddenly saw myself, and then my older sister. We had both devoted tremendous physical and emotional energy to Mother in her final weeks. I knew that came more naturally to me than to her, for my relationship with Mother had always remained on a positive plane.

Not so for my sibling. She and Mother practically began her life at odds with one another. Unlike Cornelia, my sister had not spent a lifetime living with her mother, nor could she ever have been forced to. One of Mother's favorite lines about her eldest daughter was that she never knew the meaning of the word *no*. The family mythology included tales of ropes placed around refrigerator doors to prevent my older sister's search for raw eggs as a toddler. No matter the punishment, she returned repeatedly to the delight of cracking eggs open and spilling their contents onto the floor, then scooping up the yoke and carrying it away to various locations. The discovery of an aged raw egg yolk presented problems of its own, but worse was the effect of the invisible slippery egg whites on the leather soles of the hapless person who next walked into the kitchen.

In a world before cleverly designed toddler restraints, my wayward sister was tethered by a restraining rope around her waist while my harried mother attempted to hang wash. At first, the diminutive escape artist was attached to a red wagon. She departed the yard at a run, the wagon-in-tow raising a noisy alarm throughout the neighborhood. In Mother's next hopeful maneuver, bricks were added to the wagon's bed for weight. My sister regarded this handicap, as she would all physical or emotional loads throughout her lifetime, many of which she blamed directly on her mother, as one more challenge that she would conquer. Their early conflict of wills marked a lifelong relationship for mother and daughter that resulted in my sister's teen years being filled with screaming theatrics on her part and mounting frustration on my mother's. When my sister reached adulthood, the strain sparked lengthy silences from time to time between the two. Mother found fault; daughter rose to the bait. As I read again Ellen Weatherall's comments to herself about her children, "There they were, made out of her, and they couldn't get away from that," I think of how hard my older sister tried to get away.

But with Mother's impending death came an unexpected opportunity for their release from the grip of their long-standing disagreements. Our brother lived a couple of states away; he had visited often during the past weeks, but couldn't move in to provide the round-the-clock care required. Our younger sister was suffering through her own nightmare of breast cancer and chemotherapy, a battle that left her too frail to assume trying duties. So during Mother's last six weeks, my sister and I took turns staying with her. I lived out of state, but only a six-hour drive away, a drive that had become quite familiar as I traveled back and forth multiple times during what would obviously be Mother's final year of life. At first, the clash between my mother's and sister's titan wills continued; the long-established roles were just too hard to change. Then gradually, an alteration occurred. This happened when my sister at last managed to convince Mother that she needed full-time care, care in which she intended to participate. Our mother's acquiescence, possibly for the first time in their history, to her daughter's opinion on an issue of importance shifted their relationship.

I felt a thrill of relief when my sister told me she would help stay with Mother, but also heavy doubt. Unlike my other, scientifically minded siblings, one a nurse and one a biochemist, this sister has the personality of an artist. A musician, trained at the Eastman School of Music, she has never easily borne a sick room; I remember the problems she had, despite her tremendous capacity for love, in dealing with even her children's illnesses. Cancer is not gentle in its final stages, and she would be called upon to engage in some very unpleasant activity. But in those last weeks, both women came to terms with seemingly unsolvable problems. My sister magnificently rose beneath the physical and psychological demands placed on her shoulders, and my mother expressed aloud her appreciation, perhaps cherishing her daughter's love in a way she'd not been able to before.

Other aspects of the character of Granny Ellen Weatherall bring my mother to mind. One of those is the character's take-charge attitude—her ability, symbolically indicated by her name, to weather all storms—and the constant edicts she issues: "I want you to pick all the fruit this year and see that nothing is wasted. There's always someone who can use it. Don't let good things rot for want of using. You waste life when you waste good food. Don't let things get lost. It's bitter to lose things." Raised during the Depression, my mother too lacked any tolerance for waste. She came close to measuring one's morality by the amount of food wasted in the home. And she always had advice about better ways of doing things. Often she was right. Still, no one wanted to listen—not to advice that sounded too close to criticism from a mother who always seemed so sure of herself.

One time Mother insisted that if I chose a different setting for my car's air conditioner, more efficient air circulation would result. I bristled at the idea of being told as a grown woman and mother of three how to operate my car. When she reached toward the glove box to consult the automobile manual and prove her point, I said sharply, "Don't touch that!" I hardly ever crossed my mother, and thus felt a bit intoxicated by the rebellion displayed in my outburst. She sat in silence for a moment, then said, "I feel sorry for people like you. People who don't want to learn a better way." My victory went hollow, hissing in its demise like a deflating balloon.

While Mother lay dying, I had to leave each weekend, and my sister would arrive. That May I had to attend three graduations in a row. The first weekend, I returned home to join my husband so we could attend ceremonies at the university where we both worked. After driving back to stay with my mother for several days, on the following weekend I picked up my husband so we could travel to Missouri to attend the high school graduation of my daughter. I trekked back to Arkansas until the next weekend. Then we repeated our routine, in order to attend the high school graduation of my stepson in Kansas.

Each time I returned to her apartment, I hesitated to look, really look hard, at Mother. Her physical condition deteriorated rapidly, and her weight hung stubbornly under 100 pounds. I worried that her spindly legs could not hold her, but all too soon, that no longer mattered. Later I came across a scene from *Anna Karenina* involving the death of Levin's brother. As I read Levin's reaction to his brother's appearance, I saw myself staring at Mom:

> Impossible that this terrible body can be my brother
> Nicholas, he thought. But he drew nearer, saw the face,
> and doubt was no longer possible. In spite of the dreadful
> change on the face, Levin had only to glance at those living
> eyes raised toward him . . . to understand the dreadful
> truth that this dead body was his living brother. (446)

Exhausted, I had returned home on a Monday, planning to come back to Mother the following weekend. The hospice nurse had told my sister that she believed Mom had only a couple of weeks left. Twenty-four hours later, my sister called. "I hope I'm doing the right thing," she said. "The nurse tells me that Mom looks like she may slip into a coma. If you want to speak with her again, you better come." My husband offered to drive me this time, making the point that should things go well, he could return to work, then pick me up when the end came. I wouldn't need a car while there.

By the time we made it to the apartment, Mother had not eaten anything for three days. She had begun a regular round of vomiting. My sister whispered to me that she thought she saw tissue in the basin. Although appalled, I am yet amazed at her confidence in handling the situation.

<hr/>

Like Ellen Weatherall, my mother had loved two men. Of course, she was never left at the altar, jilted as was Ellen by her first lover. Mother married and buried both of her loves, the two of whom couldn't have been more different, or so it seemed to me. I never knew my father, who died in the Korean conflict when I was an infant. Because Mother married my stepfather when I was only four, for all intents and purposes, that man was Daddy, and she spoke rarely of my genetic father until I asked about him years later. I recorded many of the stories she told me, and I have his letters, newspaper clippings about his courageous death, and many photographs. I believe they were very much in love. She could still describe decades later the intensity of her pain when she heard he'd been taken from her and their three small children at such a young age.

She told me that she had for a time looked for some sign, something to explain not only why this had happened, but how she might survive alone and raise her children. When Ellen Weatherall remembers feeling as though she were dropping "out of the world," left "blind and sweating with nothing under her feet and the walls falling away," I picture my mother, listening to the news of her husband's death from the Army officer at her door. She explained that she felt not only anger at being deserted but also guilt over that anger. I think of Elisabeth Kübler-Ross's words in her essay "On the Fear of Death":

> This grief, shame, and guilt are not very far removed from feelings of anger and rage. The process of grief always includes some qualities of anger. Since none of us likes to admit anger at a deceased person, these emotions are often disguised or repressed and prolong the period of grief or show up in other ways. (1202)

Most likely my mother experienced the same emotions at her losses that I experience now.

The tortured dreams begin about a month after her death. They include various versions of her return from the dead, at which point I panic, because we have dismantled her home. In another variation, I suddenly recall that she's alive, and realize that we have left her to die alone. In one quite vivid dream, I again sit with her as she dies. In my waking state, I have actually fantasized about having a second chance to speak with her, to say all of those things I want to tell her again. I fearfully imagine Mother in those last hours having seen me as Ellen Weatherall sees Cornelia, when her daughter "knelt down and put her head on the pillow. She seemed to be talking, but there was no sound. . . . Cornelia's mouth moved urgently in strange shapes" (1128). I fear that my own mother, because she suffered impaired hearing, had not understood my last few comments. Of course, in the dream, when my second chance comes, I can barely speak. Finally I tell her that she mustn't die, because I cannot do what I must without her. In a voice so clearly hers that for a moment I believe she stands beside my bed, she replies, "Oh, yes you will, because that's how I raised you." It is the first of many signs that I receive in the aftermath of our separation.

I read in the story that Ellen's "breath crowded down under her ribs and grew into a monstrous frightening shape with cutting edges; it bored up into her head and the agony was unbelievable; Yes, John, get the doctor now, no more talk, my time has come" (1128). The reader quickly understands that Ellen thinks not of death, but rather recalls the birth of her last child, the favorite that she would later lose. The close connection of birth to death cannot be missed in Porter's imagery.

This is how a friend explains another of my dreams to me. It's an unpleasant vision, veiled and mysterious and making little sense, as dreams will. I'm with my mother in a delivery room. Although she's far past childbearing age, her stomach swells grotesquely. Suddenly the scene jumps again to her death bed, her belly swollen by the growth that robs her, robs all of us, of her life. In the disorientation of dreams, she delivers her baby, or the tumor delivers her, and then she dies.

"It's OK," my friend says gently. "You know how some people believe that at death we undergo a rebirth of sorts? That's all it means." I recall the image of my younger, cancer-stricken sister, pale and ill from battle with an invisible enemy of her own. Silently she leaned over Mother's dead body, tentatively placing her hand on the bulge beneath Mother's skin that died along with its victim.

Like Cornelia and her siblings, we hovered close to Mother in those last days, more in communion with ourselves than in an attempt to help her. Little remained to be done.

As Ellen Weatherall confronts her death and her disappointment, she thinks, "So my dear Lord, this is my death and I wasn't even thinking about it. My children have come to see me die. But I can't, it's not time. Oh, I always hated surprises. . . . Oh, my dear Lord, do wait a minute. . . . I meant to do something" (1130).

Part way through that long night, Mother asks if I see her telephone bill. I say that it's in the other room; we'll take care of it.

A moment later she speaks haltingly. "I forgot to mail—oh, my, I think I really goofed." No, I tell her, everything is fine. Later we decide she was probably referring to a withdrawal slip she had filled out in preparation for emptying a retirement account, a move that would have prevented the paying of estate tax. Her acuity in her last hours amazes me. Even with a morphine pump repeatedly administering what I am told equals approximately 60 times a normal twenty-four-hour dosage, her mind remains clear. We are able to exchange remarks until her last moment.

I recall the visit during which the hospice nurse asks Mother to rate her pain on a scale of one to ten. Mother thinks, then replies, "Seven." When the nurse stares at her skeptically, Mom comments, "I was raised not to complain. We were taught to be stoic." The nurse replies carefully, "This is not the time." Mother hesitates, then revises her rating to a nine. I whisper to the nurse, "Twenty." When the pills no longer yield relief, Mother receives a shunt inserted into an arm vein. She can control the administration of morphine, injecting whatever she needs.

Hospice includes as part of its marvelous service a description of what to expect from a terminal patient in her final hours. I'm glad to have read it when I observe Mother begin to pick at her sheets and her gown and repeatedly reach out to rearrange the pans and box of tissue on her bedside table, activity predicted by the hospice information. For a period, her fingers rove unceasingly, touching, touching, as if the tactile sensation provided by the objects around her keeps her rooted in reality. Later I notice in *Anna Karenina,* in the description of Nicholas's death, comments by Mary Nikolavna to Levin. She says, "Today it will end, you'll see." When Levin asks why she believes this to be true, Mary explains, "He has begun to clutch at himself . . . like this." She demonstrates by plucking at the folds of her dress. Then Levin notices that Nicholas continues "catching at himself" all day long, "as if wishing to pull something off" (458).

We arrive at about 3:00 P.M. on the day after my sister's call. Obviously exhausted, she repeats herself several times. "Be sure to rub her back," she tells me, "she really likes that. They're bringing a hospital bed later, with rails. One nurse said we should think of putting a suction tube down so she doesn't have to vomit. I don't think she's in any pain now."

My younger sister and her husband are there; I'm shocked by this sister's run-down appearance. The chemotherapy treatments for her breast cancer extract their toll in human energy, in human will. She insists on staying on schedule to complete her final administration of the poisonous chemical, that Janus-faced friend/foe substance, even though her white blood cell count, and thus her level of resistance to disease, falls to a dangerous low. She battles her unseen nemesis, sibling to that enemy that slowly kills her mother.

"I don't like the idea of the suction tube," my older sister says.

I agree. "Mother wouldn't like that. She deserves her dignity. Let's wait."

I plan to stay in the one-bedroom apartment that night. When the hospital bed arrives, my husband helps the delivery men move Mother's bed into the living room, giving me a place to sleep. My sister had been dozing at night in a recliner. Incredibly, when my husband enters the bedroom, my mother calls him by name and asks after his health.

Everyone leaves. My older sister travels to her home about forty-five minutes away. My younger sister and her husband live close by, and my husband finds a motel room for the night. He tells me to call if I need him.

The next few hours become a routine of my traveling in and out of Mom's bedroom. I don't want to sleep; I fear I'll miss her call for help. I ache all over as I watch her continual retching, but she doesn't complain. She worries about a possible bad odor. I assure her none exists. All I can do is chip ice for her, which I do about once an hour. I rub her back, then lift her hand to kiss it. She pulls it away to continue its roving motion.

Empty the nastied pan, bring the clean. Replace the kicked-off covers, pat her legs. Each time she makes a noise, I run into her bedroom. "My little jack-in-the-box," she jokes with me at one point. The apartment is silent, except for the swishing of the pump as it delivers the blessed relief. She dozes intermittently, propped up on one elbow with the emesis basin close at hand. But she never loses consciousness. At one point, she twice murmurs her sister's name. I swallow hard, watching her struggle.

When she opens her eyes, I say, "You must be so tired." I want to give her permission to let go, to let her know I understand.

"You must be, too," she tells me. "Can't you get any sleep?"

I say, "I want to be with you. We love you so much. I just want to make you more comfortable." I realize the stupidity of such a remark as she smiles feebly and mutters a characteristic, "Ha."

At about 3:15 A.M., she asks for more ice. I bring it to her in the ridiculously tiny juice glass that she can handle.

"What's the date?" she asks. I grope for an answer. Recently, all the days have to run together for me.

"Oh," she answers herself, "it's June 14th."

"Right," I say, reminding her that my brother will arrive today.

"Is he flying or driving?" she asks.

When I reply, she lifts herself up on her elbows, leaning toward me. Thinking she wants the ice, I place a hand behind her head for support, and move close. But she doesn't place her lips to the glass rim. She lays her head, just for a moment, on my chest.

Then she slides down toward her pillow, but an elbow is caught under her body, preventing her lying down. As I try gently to pull her arm straight, she struggles with me, exercising an incredible strength. Then her breathing slows, and her body relaxes. I can't believe she's going to die, not now. The nurse estimated another couple of weeks. For a moment I panic, wondering whether I should run for the phone to try to summon my younger sister. But then I know there is not time.

I murmur again and again, "Mom. Oh, Mom." Her body literally winds to a stop as I sit reverently, my arms cradling her. Later my older sister tells me, "She waited for you. You know she did." All I can do is look into her eyes at her final moment. What do I see there?

⟡

Porter, like the rest of us, can only guess at what happens within as a person embraces death. She writes of Ellen Weatherall:

> Her heart sank down and down, there was no bottom
> to death, she couldn't come to the end of it. The blue
> light from Cornelia's lampshade drew into a tiny point
> in the center of her brain, it flickered and winked like an
> eye, quietly it fluttered and dwindled. Granny lay curled
> down within herself, amazed and watchful, staring at
> the point of light that was herself; her body was now
> only a deeper mass of shadow in an endless darkness
> and this darkness would curl around the light and swallow
> it up. (1131)

Granny Weatherall begs God for a sign, but one does not appear.

⟡

I only hope that my mother at last received her sign. I still think of the expression in her eyes, not of anger, nor of fear, as she gazed at something I could not see. Perhaps I witnessed an expression reflecting a wonder that must remain foreign to those left behind. I do know that one moment Mother was there, the next absent. At 3:30 in the morning, with her final breath, I watched her essence, that mysterious thing that constituted my mother, depart. I finally understood all of the references I've heard to the body as a shell, a mere casing, a discarded cocoon. At 3:31, I touched its hair, I kissed its forehead. But my mother had, one minute earlier, left the room.

                             ❦

I discovered the poetry of Rabindranath Tagore in an anthologized version of Kübler-Ross's essay "On the Fear of Death." I discuss this poem, and the essay it introduces, with freshmen literature students almost every semester. I've never really "seen" the poem until now when its voice becomes my own. It's called "Fruit-Gathering," a title that makes me think of Bradstreet's reference to the fruit harvest in her elegy to little Elizabeth Bradstreet. It reads:

> Let me not pray to be sheltered from dangers
> but to be fearless in facing them.
> Let me not beg for the stilling of my pain
> but for the heart to conquer it.
> Let me not look for allies in life's battlefield
> but to my own strength.
> Let me not crave in anxious fear to be saved
> but hope for the patience to win my freedom.
> Grant me that I may not be a coward, feeling your mercy
> in my success alone; but let me find the grasp of your
> hand in my failure.

Class discussions of this poem focus in part on the identity of the person being addressed by the poem's speaker. As expected, most students suggest God or some sort of deity as the addressee. Students note immediate parallels to the Serenity Prayer by Reinhold Niebuhr spoken by those involved with step programs, such as that used by Alcoholics Anonymous. It begins, "God grant me the serenity to . . . ," stressing the theme of acceptance, just as Tagore's poem does. Students mention that, like Niebuhr's, Tagore's speaker pleads for courage, not escape. Prior to Mother's death, I agreed with my students on a further point, that the prayer originates from one considering personal mortality. I no longer feel confident of that stance. Now the poem speaks to me of one struggling for acceptance, not of his or her own eventual death, but of that of another.

The dangers referred to in the first line represent those of denial, an action that could offer a false sense of security, for both the primary victim, one who must die, and the secondary victim, one who must accept that death. I have little trouble with the acceptance of Mother's absence in the literal sense of the term; however, I sometimes simply forget that she's gone. The urge still strikes to call her and share the news of a new book contract, an accomplishment on the part of one of my children, or my disappointment over a student's problems. The second challenge, to resist begging "for the stillness of my pain," I find more difficult. Her absence remains painful in the extreme. When I begin to think I cannot conquer that pain, she reminds me that I do have the heart for it, because that's the way she raised me.

How simple it would be to call on those "allies in life's battlefield," to build misery upon misery, never looking for a way out from under the burdens we all face. Then I remember my mother, facing her illness, fighting against seemingly invincible odds to survive emergency surgery, later beating her life-span prognosis twofold. On one of her final visits to her oncologist, the doctor expressed puzzlement that testing had not shown what she could observe with her own eyes—the growth of Mom's tumor. Mother told me later, "I'd love to fool them just one more time." It was not to be, but through no lack of trying on her part.

Yes, I want relief from the fear I share with all of us forced at some point, through the death of another, to face our own mortality. How glorious to experience freedom from fear of death, of an ending so final, so mysterious, to "not crave in anxious fear to be saved" but rather to "hope for the patience to win my freedom." My mother, practical person that she was, chose patience over a salvation she knew she could not claim. Her final near-thirteen years she spent gazing into death's visage, in whatever form it took in her mind's eye, but she never admitted to a fear of dying. It was not death, but the patience to make her way through life, especially those last few years, that required her exhibition of courage.

In addition to the challenges we all must face, she wrangled with the loss of weight and of her hair, the incredibly specialized diet that resulted from the surgical removal of a gangrenous loop of intestine, the onset of diabetes as a byproduct of her cancer, the debilitating chemotherapy that acted on her like death itself. Yet she wrote to friends in her Christmas letter, "I'm feeling good now. My cancer has been in remission for three years but it's somewhere in my body and could start causing havoc again (scans don't show it yet)." She described her activities, which included her "fascinating hobby of genealogy," duplicate bridge, PEO and church circle meetings, water aerobics from May through November, walks and "old folks' aerobics" at her church during other months. She added, "I spend a *lot* of time reading and hardly any watching T.V." That unflagging anticipation of the next year, month, week, day, hour, minute, and, at the end, breath, literally kept her alive. The progress of her life/death moved in a circular fashion, wandering occasionally afield, but always returning in a contracting spiral of time that at last collapsed in upon itself.

In the midst of struggle, she found the energy to offer me emotional and mental support during graduate studies as I tackled a late-in-life third career. I needed that support badly, as my own energy often flagged. She shared the unending grief caused by the loss of custody of my children and joined me in celebrating my second marriage and my discovery of a new life partner. She found the strength, courage, and compassion to care for my step-father as his body slowly admitted defeat to prostate cancer, burned with indignity over her youngest child's discovery of breast cancer three months after marriage, and bragged on the hanging plant I brought for her final Mother's Day: "I swear I can see it grow right before my eyes."

Tagore's final stanza unites the fragments that come before. Reading his words, I see my lack of acceptance as cowardly as I search for "mercy" in whatever limited "success" I achieve in coping with my loss. Instead, I should celebrate my failure as an opportunity to find in others that support that all humans require in order to persevere. In the last few weeks, my mother learned a difficult lesson for one always so independent when she reached for the willing hands of those who loved her, and she chose to die literally in my arms. "It was her last gift to you," my husband told me as I sought comfort in his arms later that day. She gave me many things—love for language as a path to self-awareness, appreciation for the well-turned phrase, and her comfort, abiding yet on the spiritual shelf where it waits to fill my daily needs.

Someone, whose identity I can't recall now, said that with death a life ends, but a relationship does not. The change in my relationship with my mother offers challenges. In literature, I find the ways by which others meet these challenges, and I follow suit. I write. I write for myself, but also for her, and to realize aspects of our relationship that I'd not quite grasped before.

One of Mother's letters reflected her usual gaze toward the future as she struggled over choosing a marker for our father's, and eventually her own, grave. She wrote, "I haven't been out about a tombstone yet and have no idea what they cost. I will get a double one, I think, but I don't know about the 'pots' for flowers on each side. None of you will ever live here, & after I'm gone you won't be coming to P.B. [Pine Bluff]. So *who* would put the flowers in?"

I wrote my mother a final letter just before her funeral service. As I tucked the envelope beneath the flowers draping the coffin, I thought how pleased she would be to receive this special delivery, first-class mail. The words I wrote offered minor relief from my pain, while allowing me the opportunity to sketch a promise. In part, I told her, "with the language you taught me to love, I will shape myriads of word bouquets. These will be my flowers. And in that way I will honor your memory as I can."

Today I draw ease by assuming a modest place in the elegiac tradition. I gratefully lay claim to a legacy passed along by Bradstreet and others. Uncontained by time, we unite, lamenting the loss of those we love.

CHAPTER FIVE

Romancing Ourselves

I want a hero: an uncommon want,
When every year and month sends forth a new one,
Till, after cloying the gazettes with cant,
The age discovers he is not the true one.

—Byron, *Don Juan* I.I.1–4

As I PREPARE TO WRITE a single-volume encyclopedia of literature of love and romance for use by high school and college
students, a mental review of my own ideas about, and exposure
to, (uppercase) Romance literature and (lowercase) romance literature naturally occurs. The classical concept of the Romance as
taking root in medieval tales featuring characters of legendary
stature, with some degree of emphasis on the supernatural and
the amorous, forms a foundation. From that basic idea blooms
my notion of the modern romantic plot, which might feature any
two people sharing a bond of love and struggling against in-
evitable challenges from a variety of sources. Somewhere in between those two ideas drifts that mid-ground in the historical
development of the Romance, where knights pursue courtly love,
exhibiting chivalry along the way. Its source a rather sophisti-
cated and structured oral tradition of ballads or chant fables, Romance metamorphosed into the "anything goes" modern form
of my youth and the postmodern form of today. The reading lists
I review show that contemporary students digest many of the

so-called classics that appealed to my own formative literary sensibilities. Surely though, the postmodern generation must envision romance in a light different from that in which I envisioned it as I battled puberty during the sixties. I wonder about their particular search for the elusive heroine or hero of either upper or lowercase (R/r)omance, the one that's particularly of their age, and whether she/he will one day fall victim in a postpostmodern age to what Byron so disrespectfully labels "cant."

At a first glance, contemporary younger audiences seem to have little need for that old-fashioned love and romance on which my generation cut its passion teeth. Because these young people inhabit my classroom as well as compose a portion of the audience for which I write, their ideas regarding the definition of reality, and the place of romance within that definition, remain important. Its importance to me as a teacher balances its importance to me as an individual who has found much to link feminist study, literally a means of personal salvation for me, with the postmodern idea of individual realities being shaped by outside forces.

I do not now consider myself a postmodernist, nor will I in the future, partly because I'm one of those who believes we're forever trapped in the time warp of our youthful influences. Besides, much of postmodern philosophy I find distasteful. I continue to grapple, for instance, with my own mixed feelings concerning Jean-François Lyotard's incredulity toward metanarratives, the cultural mythologies, such as religion and science, that direct the formation of our self-concepts. A particular fondness for, and dependence upon, these mythologies haunt my study of literature, a study that brings me into repeated contact with literary metanarratives such as the classical quest. My knowledge of its patriarchal construction does not reduce my appreciation for its elements, elements that reverberate through almost every plot I read.

I remain nevertheless intrigued by the inroads that some postmodern thought has made into a consideration of the effects of culture on one's identity. This particularly in light of the possibilities for overlap in feminist practice and ideas of poststructuralism, a postmodern product. Postructuralism or, more correctly, deconstruction, urges reader consideration of the origin of meaning in accepted binary oppositions such as man/woman, in which man is always privileged. But where does an awareness of the linguistic power afforded traditional patriarchally constructed oppositions like man/woman lead us? Must romance be replaced with suspicion based on our new awareness that what we thought down through the ages represented man *and* woman was really man *versus* woman? These questions threaten to derail altogether my consideration of (R/r)omance and my attempts to begin on the encyclopedia. By now, however, I know better than to ignore my mental tangents, so I embark on my own quest somehow to unite my feminist proclivities, my yet romantic self, and postmodernism's questioning of the power granted that very mythology from which the Romance tradition grew.

Definitions of self, although determined increasingly by the public sphere, represented by the media and all those messages floating out there in the miasma of cyberspace, still seem to remain affected, and affect-able, by the private realm of reading and interaction with the written words of another. Thank goodness for that, I say, in spite of a postmodernist outcry against metanarrative. Yet it seems remarkable that the tradition of romance, and the romantic self, survive. This day of mass communication, of the Internet opening up the world to all takers, hardly allows the nurturing of traditional fantasies regarding love between two members of a devoted couple. T.V. bombards watchers with dysfunctional families and parodies traditional relationships through tasteless sitcoms that invite viewers to laugh at and pity characters that may resemble themselves. In many medialized relationships, cynicism and irony replace traditional romantic warmth and respect. Today's young readers swim in a sea of public revelation of discontent; nothing remains a secret anymore. This open world has its positive aspects. Where I matured in a generation that encouraged the glossing over of damaging and unhealthy relationships with a patina of respect, the present era instead reveals all. Some secrets should not be kept, but perhaps others should. R/romance requires some mystery for survival.

Yet young people still read literature, and not just because they are forced to do so in the classroom. The allure of Romance remains, and it no longer seems to depend upon innocence or naivete in its readers. Part of this phenomenon of reading results simply from the human need for escape, and perhaps young people need escape nowadays more than ever. But how about a few years down the road, how will their definitions of self and of relationships with others alter when they remove their eyes from the page and notice what's happening around them? How have my own definitions altered since my initial exposure to Romance and, later, to romantic experiences?

<hr />

My late thirties brought to me a reckoning of sorts with my false view of romance. I always envisioned romance as an ongoing state. Not so naive that I expected my heart to gyrate in the presence of my spouse after almost two decades of marriage, I still thought that the trust and faith following romance's initial throes would indeed survive. When they did not survive, and when I almost did not survive the resultant aftermath of romance, my ideas regarding the relationships between men and women greatly altered. Idealistically, Western-style Romance, as in those idealistic tales, promised happiness in the union of a man and woman. Practically, however, romance, as in the pursuit of love in the not-so idealistic patriarchal society I inhabited, upheld its promises mainly for the man. Woe be unto that woman who still participates in the love-honor-and-obey tradition—those are promises many males take literally only in application to the female.

That realization affected my ideas about Romance as literature containing plots with elements of love. Feminism forced me into an uncomfortable realization that the question of what "it" is to be a woman had been answered (for me) by men, that men had defined (for me) femininity and sensuality, and that if I could muster the nerve, verve, and wherewithall to undertake a Penelopean task, I might redefine my self.

Suddenly I saw Romance and romantic novels not as delicious tales of passion in which to exult, but as one more tool shaping my subjection to men. This literature brainwashed me into later accepting a way of life that promised fantasy fulfillment but delivered instead the reality of the subordination of my needs, as wife and mother, to those of all others. My idea of the perfect lover represented a Byronic/white-knight figure, the perfect blend of the dark and the light. While I at once adored and was repelled by Brontë's Mr. Rochester, I also found much to recommend Austen's Mr. Knightley.

Like a multitude of my teenage sisters, I thrilled to the scene in *Gone with the Wind* where Rhett Butler in all his Byronic glory literally sweeps his protesting wife, Scarlett, off her perfect feet to rush headlong up a flight of stairs, carrying her into a night of perpetual delight. Still under Knightley's influence, I had only a vague idea of what happened with Rhett and Scarlett once the door at the top of the stairs closed. Along with the majority of the novel's readers, I wanted Scarlett to be with Rhett, so I ignored her resistance to his attentions as anything other than a sign of her obvious fickleness. Because Scarlett awoke the next morning in song, her ever-attentive Mammy close by, I had to assume that whatever happened between Rhett and Scarlett proved positive.

When I return now to review Mitchell's novel in preparation for composing my encyclopedia entry, it is Ellen O'Hara, Scarlett's mother, who catches my attention. I'm particularly moved by the early description of this character thirty-two years of age, when she was "a middle-aged woman, one who had borne six children and buried three. She was a tall woman, standing a head higher than her fiery little husband, but" (and here comes the important part—the solution to the prickly problem of a woman who stood taller than her man) "she moved with such quiet grace in her swaying hoops that her height attracted no attention to itself" (27). What a bit of magic that grace and those hoops worked on bystanders. Like blinding fairy dust, they canceled all recognition of Ellen's stature. This enduring rule of the South, that of not calling attention to one's self, caused clever girls to use the immediate geography of busy wallpaper, a little-noted corner, or a discreetly placed bench as allies in the search for anonymity. Female silence, if not golden, remained highly valued by males, particularly in a public forum.

Following a lengthy description of Ellen O'Hara's patrician appearance, Mitchell adds, "only from life could Ellen's face have acquired its look of pride that had no haughtiness, its graciousness, its melancholy and its utter lack of humor" (27). Only from a life of loss and silence. But the character did not always keep that melancholy to herself, for in Ellen's death scene, Mitchell opens her character's lips and her heart. Ellen calls out not for Gerald O'Hara, her husband through an arranged marriage, but rather for that unseen character upon whose absence the plot remains entirely dependent, the man from whom in her youth she was forced apart. Better I as a young reader had paid attention to this cautionary tale than to the promise of a night at the top of the stairs.

Instead, it was Scarlett with whom I remained enthralled. I remember discovering years later that others had shared my unexplained sense of longing for Scarlett's ultimately dissatisfying life. While working as a medical technologist in a Denver blood bank, I spoke with a donor about Mitchell's novel, though the reason for my doing so now escapes me. In the midst of our conversation, a middle-aged female co-worker sporting severely cropped gray hair who rarely ever spoke five connected words, startled me with the rapturous exclamation, "Oh, I *loved Gone with the Wind*. For years after reading that novel, I believed I *was* Scarlett!"

It was all Rhett's doing. One cannot deny his close connection to Byron's hero, his blood link to Mr. Rochester, Heathcliff, and even the suggestion of his position as elder brother to Maxim de Winter, who would appear on the literary scene a scant two years later. When Scarlett first sees Rhett, she feels forced to pull "her eyes away from his without smiling back." But we know she wants to smile, and she wants to badly. Mitchell tells us of Rhett:

> He looked quite old, at least thirty-five. He was a tall man and powerfully built, heavy with muscles, almost too heavy for gentility. When her eye caught his, he smiled, showing animal-white teeth below a close-clipped black mustache. He was dark of face, swarthy as a pirate, and his eyes were as bold and black as any pirate's appraising a galleon to be scuttled or a maiden to be ravished. There was a cool recklessness in his face and a cynical humor in his mouth as he smiled at her. (68)

The reader has a few hundred pages to anticipate the pirate's scuttling of Miss Scarlett.

───※───

Never, never, never at that stage in my life would I have construed Rhett as a rapist, and, indeed, the legal concept of marital rape did not exist either during Rhett's or Margaret Mitchell's age. Yet years later, when I faced relocation to teach at a regional university, I flinched in distaste when I discovered the school was located in the only state in our perfect union that did not yet legally protect a wife from rape by her spouse. Today's generation has grown up with an awareness of the dangers of gender inequity that I lived half a lifetime before discovering. This knowledge of women's rights must affect the manner in which youth read *"Jane Eyre"*, in which they attempt to digest Rochester's imprisonment of Bertha in the attic, and his tricking of Jane. Whatever that effect on their reading may be, it's not a destructive one, for *Gone with the Wind,* complete with scenes of white men enslaving women and blacks alike, still enjoys wide sales and popularity. My twenty-something daughter, and her younger teenage sister, are responsible for the dog-eared condition of my hardback copy of Mitchell's novel, so the appeal obviously remains.

Not quite so obvious is what women, now ready to acknowledge and deal with their marginalization in life and literature, both as readers and writers, will do with scenes of oppression that remain cloaked by the term "romantic."

The older of my daughters agrees to help me perform research for the encyclopedia, and we discuss the possible entries. She knows most of the classics ("I *still* can't take Jane Austen"), and her interest piques when I mention inclusion of contemporary writers as well. She begs me to consider including a novel by Tabitha King. I don't recognize the name.

"She's wonderful," my daughter assures me. "Her characters and conflict are really pertinent to what you like to call *my* generation." (She refuses to adopt the term Generation X, declaring its connotation of illiteracy distasteful.)

I trust her judgment, and I promise to locate the King novel, *One on One,* that she suggests.

"By the way," she adds, "Tabitha King is Stephen King's wife."

I find hopeful the fact that King's identification with her famous spouse came as a secondary consideration for my daughter.

❦

The Byronic hero, for which his namesake had so earnestly searched, has served a reading public well for decades. Of course, we have the Brontë sisters to thank in great part for his perpetuation. I recall having read that Charlotte Brontë was advised by one critic to study the work of Jane Austen in order to improve her own. Charlotte admitted to never having read Austen, but after studying *Pride and Prejudice,* she wrote that Austen lacked poetic style, reflected an overabundance of realism, and thus offered little of use. She echoed Byron's desire for something other than the "real," something to be found, to be discovered in life— maybe this provides the link to ideas of postmodern thought to which I cannot help turning a curious eye. These ideas include a skepticism toward what Richard Rorty carefully distinguishes as the uppercase-T Truth, that something that promises us knowledge of what is real and what is not (*Consequences,* xiv). When we understand that promise as futile, that reality remains contingent upon our cultural experiences, we're liberated to look beyond inherited ideas of what is real to new concepts, unconstrained by space or time. This was no trick for Charlotte Brontë, poised on the outermost edges of a British social reality that the wildness of the moors denied.

Brontë's imagined Rochester, with both black boots firmly planted on a Byronic foundation, thrilled me as a young reader. But, then again, I remember also being thrilled by plain Jane, a character with whom I could identify. In the midst of the horrific Gothic scenes in that novel, the scene that stuck in my mind was Jane's lashing out at the lord of the manor, telling him basically that he best not confuse her diminutive physical stature with the size of her passion for life. In reading *Jane Eyre,* my search for a hero divulged a (s)hero instead. It seemed an important discovery at the time, but for some reason, I relegated it to a back shelf in my consciousness.

Clearly, by the time Rhett's ardor devolved into an image of rape, many changes had taken place, both in my internal perceptions of self and in the external world's perceptions of women in general. Feminism had given all of us tools by which to alter our understanding of our private and public selves. The link between the two appeared to be one of language. Terms such as "subjectivity" and "patriarchy," new to my critical vocabulary, supplied labels for conditions long experienced. I had been convinced as a teenager, through my reading of Romance and through Christian training, that my own identity depended on my service to others. This important aspect of the metanarrative of religion with which I matured catches the attention of Rorty. He writes concerning beliefs of the metaphysician, or religious person, that "perfect self-realization can be attained through service to others." Departing an eighteen-year marriage about twenty years after my teen stage, I no longer envisioned that service as leading to the community Rorty discusses. An ideology of commonality between all humans unites the community of true believers to which he refers (*Contingency,* xiii). Rorty offers this idea as an example of a failed ideology, and I strongly agree with his assessment. Echoes of my pastor's advice to "be a good wife" (translate, *serve*) and to "turn the other cheek" (add, *again*) in a clearly disastrous and damaging marriage still linger in my mind. When my romantic fantasy dissolved into so much dust, I had only my own choices to blame. Several more years would pass before I realized why I had made those choices.

The patriarchal community that benefited from my service seemed to rank my nature below its own. In reaction to bitter disappointment and distrust, I felt myself turn from one metanarrative, that of religion, to another, an antisocial Nietzschean philosophy that insists that within our selves exists no "sense of human solidarity," but rather ideas produced by a process of socialization. My admission of the truth of that insistence I found chilling, but I could hardly ignore the evidence of its pertinence to my own life. Now, as I continue years later to learn more about my self and the world, I observe Rorty urging us to accept both views, the metaphysical and the antisocial, applying each, as if specialized tools, when needed (*Contingency,* xiv).

My suspicion of the postmodern view as bereft of a moral center does not abate, but Rorty's idea of the "liberal ironist," one who abhors cruelty and admits the contingency of her beliefs and ideals, remains appealing. His vision of a "liberal utopia" reflecting a universal ironism holds promise, particularly for one who desires to cling to literature and its premise that any and all things remain possible. This utopia, founded on a concentrated effort to dismiss prejudice in all its forms, to produce a solidarity that may be achieved through imagination, rather than through inquiry, will allow all who participate a vision of one another, not as different, but as linked through our suffering. The redescription of our selves as a group that is inclusive, rather than exclusive, will depend on language.

Because I've experienced for myself the proof of this power of language, seen it work in the lives of women both to their detriment and their advantage, I must give some credence to the idea. As Rorty explains, "fiction like that of Dickens, Olive Schreiner, or Richard Wright gives us the details about kinds of suffering being endured by people to whom we had previously not attended. Fiction like that of Choderlos de Laclos, Henry James, or Nabokov gives us the details about what sorts of cruelty we ourselves are capable of, and thereby lets us redescribe ourselves" (*Contingency,* xvi). This idea of redescription I like.

The woman who declares herself of the postmodern age no longer bears the burden of seeking some predetermined reality; she may instead become involved in a process of creating knowledge, a knowledge of a "reality" that fits her individual purposes. I encounter such a process in writing autobiographical literary criticism, an approach allowing me to arrive at a very personal narrative, a reflection of my own purposes and contexts. This approach, at first glance, dovetails nicely with ideas of feminism. But herein lies the recently much-discussed rub: feminism is an active political movement, while postmodern philosophy seems to promote passivity. Poststructuralism, as a subset of postmodernism, helpfully offers a deconstruction of unified subjectivity, that darling of humanism, into fragmented subject positions. Thus we can reread Rhett as rapist and Scarlett as victim. But it also leaves humans as little more than passive puppets, unable to act as agents to help transform their cultures. One wonders how valuable postmodern assumptions regarding "what constitutes oppression and freedom," by suggesting "suspension of all forms of value judgement, of concepts such as truth, freedom and rationality," may be used in correcting the inequities it addresses (McNay, 1). Perhaps Rorty's redescription offers that mode of correction, at least on a personal level, that concerns McNay and others. It places control in the hands of the previously powerless. It allows victims to use the same tool to create for themselves a new reality that had been used to entrap them within an old.

Recent reading regarding this postmodern generation, and the postmodern ideas that it postulates, makes me think that the Romance tradition I continue to revere is but a subset of what Foucault calls the epistemes of "Myth and similitude." Foucault finds these epistemes, or metanarratives, restrictive in the understanding of truth, but that does not necessarily mean basic theories about Romance have been dismissed from the postmodern brain. Along with other critics, I envision postmodern thought as focusing on a basic concern for the expansion of possibilities within, and even the purposes for, theoretical practice (Mourad, 3). Nothing should be jettisoned; everything should be embraced.

Patricia Waugh speaks to many of my own concerns. She reflects on postmodernism's mediation of "a disintegration of belief in the full humanist subject" through "its suggestion that textuality is the primary 'reality' of a world and a book fabricated through discourse" (2). She questions whether feminist writers of fiction will or can join postmodern fictionists in their shaping of narrative that explodes a myth of the "full" character. After all, women exist as part of those marginalized, part of that Other, who "may never have experienced a sense of full subjectivity in the first place. They may never have identified with that stable presence mediated through the naturalizing conventions of fictional tradition" (2).

Great grist for the mill, indeed. How can we give up a tradition in which we have yet to participate? Waugh suggests that groups placed within society's margins by the culture dominating that society have held for generations "as a major aspect of their self-concept" identity built, not on what the postmodernist rejects as "the reflection of an inner 'essence,'" but rather on "impersonal and social relations of power." This aspect of what she terms the postmodernist "manifesto" is not news to women. Women have long understood fictional characters, not by comparison with "real people," but rather "by perceiving them through the generic and historical conventions that constitute" the female understanding of "character" at that particular moment (2).

Waugh describes one intersection of interests between postmodernism and feminism as, in part, "a concern about . . . relationships of alienation within a consumer society." She also sees both postmodernism and feminism as concerned with "the expansion of technological and scientific modes of knowledge which cannot be contained within traditional moral paradigms" (6). In other words, both approaches regard as troubling the fact that our materialistic culture continues to push minorities or groups without power farther from its social and economic center. In addition, feminism and postmodernism both express concern over those changes in technology and science that continue to expand our understanding beyond the limits our morality can handle. I think, for example, of the recent successes in the cloning of mammals, which have heightened tensions regarding scientific ethics, or even questioned the existence of ethics in science.

The first concern relates to the dearth of female voices in the development of postmodern social commentary. Waugh notes that an accounting for the comparative absence of females from the debates framed by postmodernism in the 1960s and 1980s remains a complex procedure, necessitating reflection on "economic, social, psychological, political, and aesthetic factors." But one important reason for that omission, and the point on which her entire discussion hinges, is that while postmodernism forges an

> identity through articulating the exhaustion of the existential belief in self-presence and self-fulfillment and through the dispersal of the universal subject of liberalism, *feminism* (ostensibly, at any rate) is assembling its cultural identity in what appears to be the opposite direction. . . . [W]omen writers are beginning, for the first time in history, to construct an identity out of the recognition that women need to discover, must fight for, a sense of unified selfhood, a rational, coherent, effective identity. (6)

I take her statement to mean that women have not yet found what might be termed their "selves." We must make this modern discovery first, before abandoning it for a postmodern approach to writing. If Waugh surmises correctly, my search for a postmodern presentation of romance read in classrooms written by a female will likely come to naught. Now I wonder whether I can possibly discover a male-authored novel with postmodern leanings that offers examples of women exhibiting that "selfhood," or some nascent emergence toward the type of "effective identity" to which Waugh refers.

Lengthy discussions of the meaning for education of postmodern assertions have occupied my husband and me recently as he pursues dissertation work on this very topic. One particular thought that I find applicable to my own situation is that our knowledge remains to some extent conditioned by those cultural/social mores that direct our public discourse. In other words, I may not even recognize very specific societal beliefs that shape the ideas behind the words I write and share with the public. I worry, then, about what I will teach young minds regarding romance through the encyclopedia. We discuss that writing project as presenting, in part, historical information, and the fact that the entries offer analyses, not guidelines for behavior. Still, the encyclopedia will take its very small place within the educational framework of our young adults. I wonder whether the door of my own intellect might swing wide enough to admit and face a postmodern challenge to encourage in my readers the pursuit of ideas disconnected from a particular reality composed of specific "things to know" (Mourad, 3). Suddenly, my challenge as a writer overlaps that of an educator, to say nothing of its bleed into my liberal feminist convictions.

I first think of composing the encyclopedia as a response to a notice in the section of a writer's newsletter concerning publishers' needs. This particular publisher specializes in "nonfiction on contemporary world issues and reference books (encyclopedias and biographical dictionaries) for libraries mainly at the high-school level." When I request information, I receive a letter from the senior acquisitions editor with the opening address "Dear Author," thanking me for my interest and pointing out the enclosed catalogues listing the house's previously published works. He explains that most ideas issue from an editor, who then finds the appropriate writer to execute those ideas: "many of our books are written by scholars. When I come up with a topic, I need to decide whether it can be handled by a generalist or should be written by an expert in the field." His letter encourages me to examine the enclosures and contact him when I find a topic of interest.

While the publications list impresses me, I do not see anything with which I immediately identify. When the editor calls a few weeks later, I have pretty much dismissed that project from my mind. But as he mentions certain background information from my vita, trying to match my experience to prospective projects, he again stimulates my thoughts. He explains that his company specializes in "A-Z reference books," and that his particular area of specialty encompasses a literary companion series, composed of single-volume encyclopedias that feature particular types of literature. Already-published encyclopedias include volumes about traditional epic literature, Utopian literature, allegorical literature, and satirical literature. Individual encyclopedia entries consist of four types: author, book, main characters, and concepts or necessary terms. He hopes to direct the writing of additional volumes covering social reform/protest literature, sports litera- ture, animal literature . . . and romance/confession literature. Here, he pauses, obviously hoping I'll take the bait. I do. I learn I'll need to complete a "canned" proposal form that he will supply and begin to compile about 350 listings.

The arrival of the proposal form provoked many questions. Some major questions had already been answered, the main one being how I was to determine the works to include. I learned that only novel-length works were considered, and I would choose from among those included on lists of most-often read novels by high school and college students. That information immediately placed a number of restrictions on me, some of which were wel- come. I had at first staggered under the responsibility of choosing the "correct" works, those "best representative" of (R/r)omance literature for inclusion. The task remained challenging, even though it now focused on novels only, for this particular subject matter was not as easily pinned down as that in some of the pub- lisher's other study companion categories. After all, all subgenres of novel-length fiction, from historical to science fiction, contain themes of love and romance.

A viewing of television programs such as those on MTV, geared to the group that contains my target audience, alerts me to prob- lems discussed in critical detail nowadays in reference to Gen- erations X and Y. These generations' afflictions include, according to the experts, short-term attention span linked with an incapac- ity to adopt a long-term view. Commentators on things post- modern actually use MTV, with its rapid-fire imagery and lack of depth, and movies such as *Pulp Fiction,* with its nonlinear plot presentation, as examples supporting the idea that late-twentieth-century youth, as the audience for these works, represents a postmodernish generation.

I think of the *Pulp Fiction* characters portrayed on the screen by Uma Thurman and John Travolta and of their night together on the town. Travolta's hit man character ends up plunging a six-inch needle into the Thurman character's heart, injecting the epinephrine necessary to jump-start her pump following an accidental heroin overdose. I mentally search for any relationship between Travolta's dragging Thurman across the lawn into his dealer's house for resuscitation, and Rhett's carrying Scarlett up the stairs in hopes of rejuvenating her passion. Both scenes turn on affairs of the heart, but there the resemblance seems to end. Perhaps the *Pulp Fiction* scene represents an example of the postmodern "collage" approach to art in which the ultimate original work no longer exists as a possibility. Instead, creations represent a mimetic amalgam of all that has come before, with old ideas presented in an ironic or even parodic manner.

In *Postmodernist Fiction,* Brian McHale discusses the manner by which postmodern writers foreground "ontological concerns" that represent a commonality for that group. His definition of ontology is "a theoretical description of *a* universe" (27, emphasis added). The use of "a" in place of "the" remains all important here, for the ontology may describe any universe. Quentin Tarantino's foregrounding in *Pulp Fiction* of postmodern elements through his view of an underworld universe fits this category. Obviously, I needn't concern myself with such elements in classic works (a troublesome term in itself) that focus on love and romance as themes, but what of the more (post)modern? On the lists of works read in the high-school and college classroom that challenge traditional ideas regarding romance, I spot some by Margaret Atwood and Isaac Bashevis Singer, both of whom frame their plots in cultural concepts that fall outside traditional Romance theory but that still contain themes of love and romance.

My target audience likely remains familiar with Atwood's dystopic ideas regarding romance through the film presentation, if they've not read the novel, of *The Hand Maid's Tale,* so they'll likely be prepared for my inclusion of her *The Robber Bride,* with its inversions of traditional romantic characterizations. Singer's diasporan *Enemies: A Love Story,* also available in a film version, remains grounded in the fears of isolation and death resulting from the Holocaust horror. Young readers familiar with events of the Holocaust bring to the novel some identification with situation. The eventual assumption by Singer's anti-hero, Herman Broder, of the traditionally female role of victim offers rich situational irony easily recognized. But my editor has suggested that I include a few writers not so familiar to young readers; he asks if I know much of V. S. Naipaul. I must admit that I know little.

I like the idea of including a Naipaul novel in my encyclopedia, as I've heard much of this award-winning author. Now I'll have the opportunity to become familiar with the man and his work. However, my vague knowledge of his writing makes me think that his works reflect a social and political bent that may preclude any evidence of (R/r)omance. I find a novel written quite early in his career, *The Suffrage of Elvira* (1958), and begin to read. Later I find Naipaul mentioned in a discussion by John Rothfork of Rorty's brand of postmodern thought. Rothfork mentions Naipaul as one whose advice "for the moralists and prophets is to learn a second language; to quit praying and preaching" and to turn to things more substantial to improve a third world economy (24). This statement suggests that the value of religious metanarrative should be questioned in one's search for "reality." Hm-m-m. Very postmodern.

My daughter dutifully locates for me critical materials about Naipaul and his works. He's now been writing for forty years, and twenty-two books later, his approach has changed. If not a postmodern writer, as I interpret his statements about his craft, he does seem at least to see himself as writing in a postmodern world:

[T]he literary novel is delivering, nowadays, a kind of minor extravaganza itself, with, sometimes, major personal display. The idea of pinning down reality isn't really there. It's migrated perhaps to other forms. Perhaps something like the essay will give people reality about our confused, mixed world. . . . We should rethink all forms, not only fiction; academic work, history and travel books especially. (qtd. in Hussein, 3)

One reviewer writes of Naipaul's *A Way in the World* (1995) that it lacks a "unifying thread of time or place," and claims "its nine-part scheme of biographical reminiscence, historical fable, and portraiture of imaginary-real figures, [is] consistently 'voiced' in such a way as to assure us we can trust the narrator. Sink or swim is more like it, and a number of times I sank" (Pritchard). I'm intrigued, and I eagerly anticipate learning of Naipaul's town of Elvira and its suffrage. But I wonder whether I'm trying to force contemporary writing into a mold, that of Romance or even romance, that it simply will not fit.

Now I'm really in trouble, having muddled, even contaminated, my ideas regarding Romance instead of clarifying them. I return to Rorty's suggestion that the use of language as a measure allows us to evaluate seemingly contradictory and competing literary theories simply on their effectiveness as an explanatory tool (Barringer). If I can accept this thought, then my own use of language generates meaning and a possible truth in my interpretation, as reader, of text. I can revisionarily relate the traditional idea of a novel containing multiple readings to the postmodern idea of new meanings arising from interaction between any reader's theory and that novel.

I visualize multiple single readers melding together in a community of (R/r)omance readers, whose agreement on beliefs and ideals that promote common actions becomes knowledge. That action could be the joy or tightness in the chest inspired in some readers by certain words; this type of knowing requires no theory for legitimization (Mourad, 3). The common ground on which any inquiry is based remains all important to Rorty's brand of postmodernism. So, then, the (R/r)omance reader's emotional reaction to what she reads acts as a form of knowledge, reflecting her intimate interaction with another's words.

This brings me back, always back, to the idea of language and its shaping power. Rorty discusses Romanticism as growing from an eighteenth-century idea that "truth was made rather than found," developed on the French Revolution's example that "the whole vocabulary of social relations, and the whole spectrum of social institutions, could be replaced almost overnight" (*Contingency*, 5). Naturally I remain familiar with the Romantic poets' claim for art, not as a product of imitation, but rather as the culmination of self-realization; in the back of my mind lingers the definition of poem, of which I was first made aware in graduate school, as a "thing made," from the Greek term *poiema*. Rorty translates the basis of Romantic thought into the idea that the Truth cannot be "out there" separate and apart from our concepts of self, which are shaped through language, an idea to which he grants much value. Truth "cannot exist independently of the human mind—because sentences cannot so exist. . . . [T]he world is out there, but descriptions of the world are not. Only descriptions of the world can be true or false" (*Contingency*, 5). Later, he adds, "the world does not speak. Only we do" (6).

If Rorty is right, if one's self remains the creation of human vocabulary, then feminists must surely be considered among the most prolific revisionists of language and, by extension, of the selves that language produces, of the twentieth century. Interestingly enough, Rorty himself unwittingly supplies an example of feminist influence on linguistic meaning. The incident I have in mind occurred in "The Necessity of Inspired Reading," which appeared in *The Chronicle of Higher Education*, 9 February 1996.

Rorty begins with his praise of the experience of "losing" one's self in art, of the marvelous surrender we feel to another's ideas, precisely because they are also our own. Rorty reaps trouble for himself by confessing his own "seduction" through interaction with literature. A respondent to Rorty's Point-of-View essay points out that Rorty's "act of surrender" remains power's privilege, available only to those who are "strong and protected." Our modern sensibilities remind us that those not protected by membership in a privileged group must remain on the lookout to arm themselves against any "hidden agenda or aggression on the part of the seducer," an "insight" that this particular respondent credits to feminism. He points out that women who must remain "conscious" of a fine line "between seduction and rape" will find Rorty's image problematic (Whiteis). I see Whiteis's point, and I agree that words remain powerful tools in an ongoing structuring of gender equity. At the same time I know of Rorty's "act of surrender" to literature from my own reading experience. This aesthetic and intellectual act of surrender to something better than ourselves, to Homer's idea of the "sublime," replenishes and distinguishes me. I find little relation between Rorty's reference and the physical invasion and resultant diminution of self with which Whiteis is concerned.

How can one not be intrigued by Rorty's idea that considerations of language contingency, and thus contingency of conscience, "lead to a picture of intellectual and moral progress as a history of increasingly useful metaphors rather than of increasing understanding of how things really are" (*Contingency*, 9)? If we can only compare various languages and/or metaphors to one another to reach meaning, I have merely to compare nineteenth-century metaphors for (R/r)omance with those of the twentieth century to locate the differences and/or similarities for which I search. For the moment, I see myself a member of the "made thing" camp, aligned with those who champion metaphors: "Whereas the metaphorical looks irrelevant to Platonists and positivists, the literal looks irrelevant to Romantics. For the former think that the point of language is to represent a hidden reality which lies outside us, and the latter thinks its purpose is to express a hidden reality which lies within us" (19). I've already ventured into the cosmos of society in search of an identity "out there" somewhere. Now I'm ready to turn instead to an investigation of the inner space of self.

The encyclopedia editor contacts me again, and I speak to the problem of featuring only novel-length works in the encyclopedia. How can I legitimately exclude dramatic works, such as those of Shakespeare, and epic poetry, such as that of Homer, of seminal importance in introducing plot lines that appear repeatedly in nineteenth- and twentieth-century novels?

"A solid introduction could take care of that," the editor explains. "Discuss there some of the historically important works that laid down the rules for those that followed. You'll also need to explain your criteria for selection of works. Some readers will be disappointed not to find certain of their favorite novels included, and you'll explain the reasons for exclusion. Your criteria are really important to librarians, our true market base."

My mind now experiences flight, and the possibility of lending shape to this rather amorphous thing representing love and romance literature seems feasible.

"As for important poetry," he continues, "handle that as you want. You could do one big entry just for poetry, for example."

Before he hangs up, I return to a lingering doubt. "You at first called this an encyclopedia of romance/confession literature. Does this mean we'll include works of popular romance?" I think of euphemisms—the bodice ripper, the rape epic—for what remains a genre of questionable quality in the world of academe.

"No," he answers. "This book will, after all, offer an understanding of classroom reading on the high-school and undergraduate level. Popular romances usually aren't studied there, are they? You might include a single entry discussing it as, well, the stepsister of real romance literature."

Stepsister?

"Just stick with the classics, or any books you recognize as classics-to-be."

∗∗∗

I spend a great deal of time considering possible works to cover in the encyclopedia. Burdened by my editor with the task of predicting future classics, I also ruminate, long and noisily, to anyone who will listen, over this problem. I hesitate, as appointed scholar, lest my selections reveal the less-than-scholarly emotional effects those same works had on me as a young reader. Part of me longs for that time of innocence when, untouched by any theoretical approaches to literature, and as yet unjaded by life, I could simply react to words and their resultant imagery. Suddenly I'm jealous of my prospective audience, a nonscholarly group whose members may come away from a novel inspired and forever changed by the unrestrained way ideas sparked by the reading could be appropriated to alter their own self-constructed vision.

I think again of Longinus's "On the Sublime," in which he writes of Homer's idea: "for that is really great which bears a repeated examination, and which it is difficult or rather impossible to withstand, and the memory of which is strong and hard to efface" (Bressler, 17). I wonder if we yet honor his definition of "classic" writing as that to which we will repeatedly return. I can't deny that, although armed with new ideas of female subjectivity, I remain attracted to, and read often, the (R/r)omance. According to Longinus, Homer believed that "Nature . . . implants in our souls the unconquerable love of whatever is elevated and more divine than we" (17). Admittedly, these classical ideas remain a part of postmodernism's epistemes, those oppressing and oppressive metanarratives to be resisted in our search for

Truth, but they retain their seductive quality even for those of us who have been warned.

⚜

Continued reading of Richard Rorty allows the discovery of much common ground between his and my own ideas, and I become more optimistic about addressing a postmodern audience on what seems a decidedly nonpostmodern subject. Perhaps one reason for my attraction to Rorty is the recognition of some of my own contradictory thinking in his. On first exposure, I cuddle up to his assertion that an ironist will recognize the contingency of language and also literature's power to provide tools we need to refashion our own public language into one more nearly akin to our private. He contrasts views of the metaphysician (my former self?) with those of the ironist (my present self?) in asserting that the former "thinks of the high culture of liberalism as centering around theory" while the latter "thinks of it as centering around literature." Literature, Rorty explains, includes "(in the older and narrower sense of that term—plays, poems, and especially novels)" (*Contingency*, 93).

But I see trouble looming in the shape of challenge by another part of my new self to this idea of "literature." What of the early writings by women that have so captured my imagination for the last several years? What of nontraditional literature, such as diaries and journals, so crucial to feminist studies? What of Native American literature, or any of those works not included in academe's approved canon? What of that *stepsister* that provides a whopping 51 percent of paperback sales to today's popular market readers? I see my concerns regarding Rorty's exclusive approach echoed by others. There seem to be three problems with such a restriction: Rorty never really explains why such a restriction is necessary; the obvious partiality Rorty and other literary scholars would have to such a restriction; and the exclusion of other genres which may expand an ironist's knowledge of the world (Barringer). But as I think further on Rorty's views, I believe that I, and others, may have misjudged him. For his assertion that the liberal ironist thinks the task of the intellectual to be to "increase our skill at recognizing and describing the different sorts of little things around which individuals or communities center their fantasies and their lives" (*Contingency*, 93) seems to open the door to embrace a wide variety of writings.

Following my divorce, I experimented with different kinds of writing, sorting what sells from what doesn't. I don't know now how I hit on the idea of writing for romance/confession magazines. I don't recall reading them when young, although I was aware of their existence and their categorization as soft porn. Such categorization was supported by scenes from movies in which girls thrust those publications under their mattresses when authority figures entered the private domain of the teen bedroom.

As I considered various writing venues, the confessionals caught my attention not for their rate of pay, ranging from a meager three to five cents per word, but rather for the length of stories allowed. Most of the rare magazines that still accepted unsolicited fiction for pay required lengths less than 2,000 words. These confessionals would accept up to 10,000 words, novella length. If such a story was a fast write, one could earn a respectable pay check. Thus began my relationship with one particular confessional. Over the next two years, that magazine accepted sixteen of my stories; my Christmas stories appeared three years running. I earned a bit in excess of $6,000, all told.

That I write of this experience in past tense reflects my having severed that productive relationship. I stopped writing confessionals for a couple of reasons. One was simple pragmatics; a new editor took over the task of heading the magazine that had considered me a preferred author, and she seemed not to care so much for my stories. That gave me the excuse I needed to stop, and it bolstered my second reason to do so: boredom had set in. The stories are formulaic, and I tired of repeatedly writing the same story in various guises.

However, lest anyone believe there's nothing to writing formula confessionals, I should clarify some of the challenges. The stories are printed without byline, in order to preserve their autobiographical facade. Each is written in first person and is a "true" story; they have to remain absolutely believable. Each one-page acceptance sheet mailed to me by an editor that listed a tentative publication date and payment rate also contained a brief statement of authenticity. I had to verify by signature that the events depicted had actually happened to me or were based on true stories I had heard. I'll never forget calling the publisher once and speaking to an editorial assistant who greeted me with "I've wanted to talk to you forever! I can't believe the life you've led. First you were almost date-raped and then there was that story about you working for the wealthy older woman and hitting it off with her grandson!" My guilt twinge eased when she added, "When I told my boss that I couldn't believe anyone had such an exciting life, she did mention that some of this *might* be made up." Because all stories are based on truth, character names are always changed. As a senior editor explained to me, the magazines had been sued in the past for defamation of character. Even after such changes became routine, my gestalt still suffered when I saw my "Susan" appear in published print as a "Tiffany."

The magazine's editorial guidelines printed in *The Writer's Market* read, in part, as follows: it "publishes first-person short stories on actual occurrences" covering "such topics as love, romance, crime, family problems and social issues. The magazine's primary audience consists of working-class women in the South, Midwest and rural West. Our stories aim to portray the lives and problems of 'real women.'" I considered this idea of truth and reality long and hard. There existed readers out there, lots of them if the circulation estimate of 200,000 carried any weight, who believed all those stories could be true. That remained essential to their projecting themselves into the plot. The stories must be realistic and yet juicy enough to provide fantasy material.

Not until much later did I intellectualize the fact that most of my confessional heroines both reflected *and* ruptured typical cultural conceptualizations of females. I don't think I felt myself on a personal crusade to encourage revolutionary acts among my readers; I'd not yet reached the stage of consideration of self in my personal life to support that kind of activity. But to break the monotony of plot, I tried to add what I thought of as my soapbox line to each story, something that would carry a (admittedly at times heavy-handed) social message. In one story, the heroine/victim suffered sexual harassment at the hands of a college professor, and her reaction demonstrated for readers the steps that could be taken to halt such treatment. Long before earning a minor in English that would propel me toward graduate school, I emphasized some of my favorite books in my stories. I think of the rags-to-riches story, mentioned by the editorial assistant, which featured a poverty-stricken young woman who procured a job with a wealthy patroness. Part of her duties involved reading aloud to her employer; *Pride and Prejudice* was the novel of choice. I wove ideas from the novel throughout the story as the heroine falls in love with the wealthy grandson of her employer. All the stereotypes remained easy to identify, but so did embedded messages encouraging the possibility of change. From emotional abuse to homelessness to poverty among women—all these themes appeared with my emphases in a form of fiction traditionally designed to promote female subjectivity. Faced with enormous changes in my environment, I tried to offer hints, however weak, for other women readers, as to ways by which they could alter attitudes toward their own.

I complete the exhausting task of organizing a list of topics, titles, characters, and authors to accompany my encyclopedia proposal, setting tentative deadlines to stretch over the next two years, then I send the package to my editor. Authors include Allende, Atwood, Austen, Brontë, Buck, Cather, Chopin, Conroy, Cooper, Dickens, Dreiser, du Maurier, Dumas, Esquivel, Fielding, Fitzgerald, Flaubert, C. S. Forester, E. M. Forster, Fowles, Gaines, Hardy, Hawthorne, Hemingway, Hugo, Hurston, James, Kundera, Lawrence, García Márquez, Maugham, McCullough, Mitchell, Morrison, Naipaul, Oz, Pasternak, Scott, Shelley, Singer, Styron, Tan, Thackeray, Tolstoy, Tyler, Waugh, Wharton. Over the next few weeks we work to fine-tune the list to reflect more of the multicultural bent that the editor wants; it expands with the addition of Berto, Giono, Heath, Iyayi, Kincaid, Mishima, Osaragi. This expansion makes me nervous; I'm unsure that our choices will coincide with those readings considered popular in the foreign markets targeted by my publisher. My worries don't include concerns over a lack of (R/r)omantic themes; those seem to abound in any culture's literature.

More weeks pass before I receive a brief response. He writes, "We discussed your proposal at our meeting, and although everyone likes the idea, my boss instituted a new policy, effective with that meeting: have proposals read by an outside reader. Therefore, we'd like you to have your final proposal . . . looked over by an outside reader, another academic, whose expertise is in this type of literature. Jackie Collins, Erica Jong?? Is this going to be a hassle? Please let me know your sentiments."[1]

I accept his request for my sentiments at less than literal value and decide not to share with him my true thoughts when I consider the definite hassle he suggests. Worrisome logistics will be involved and will cause yet another delay in contract negotiations. But I'm also amused and bemused by his attempt at humor that touches on the questions I've recently considered. An implication concerning those bothersome boundaries between "legitimate" and "illegitimate" literature springs off the page with the mention of "this type of literature" and the allusion to Collins and Jong as a connotative contrast. His choice of ironic examples indicates that our project remains at odds with various types of popular literature, those stepsiblings that many academics regard with disdain, if they regard them at all. And I wonder if he actually equates Collins, whom I perceive as writing sensational fluff, to Jong, an author whose writing has featured legitimate feminist issues. More germane to my turmoil than questions of quality writing is that something *happens* to people when they read novels, even to a postmodern generation that, like all of us who came before, remains needy.

The phone rings as I meditate. It's the younger of my two daughters, who now enjoys officially the status of college sophomore.

"Hey, Mom. What's up?"

"Just the same old grind. And what are you doing to celebrate your summer break?"

"I'm reading *Jane Eyre.*"

She explains she's just now had time to sit down with the hardback copy of Brontë's novel that she requested as a gift last Christmas. I flash back many years; she must be about five years old. We watch together a BBC version of *Jane Eyre,* a miniseries that appears over several nights. I cannot believe the sustained fascination on the part of my kindergartner, particularly when this version remains faithful to Brontë's challenging diction. Night after night, she cuddles close, at first in my lap, then snuggled under my arm. Only when she was about sixteen years old did she confess that the show had terrified her. Upstairs in bed each night, she had listened for sounds in her own attic. But she could hardly wait for each subsequent installment.

My recent review of Ellen Brown's personal critical piece, "Between the Medusa and the Abyss: Reading *Jane Eyre,* Reading Myself," re-exposed me to her statement, "I keep rereading

Jane Eyre and revising myself" (225). I identify with that idea, and I enjoy again her story of passing along to other reading females a tattered copy of Brontë's novel that its various female readers had signed. As my daughter reads the novel for the first time, I reread it, probably for the fifth or sixth time, to write of its characters for my encyclopedia. I wonder to whom my daughter will pass her appreciation for those same characters as I look again at Brown's paragraph regarding her teaching of the novel. She writes, in part, of her hopes for her students:

> I wanted my students to greet the novel as more than just a "good read"—something that equates it with the transience and superficiality of a "good lay." I want them to see paradigms of how to live and not to live; I want them to see choices; I want them to identify with the characters and learn from them. Choosing to teach *Jane Eyre* is a political act. (233)

Yes, we're all needy. Perhaps that's the key, and it is in the reading community, in our sharing favorite stories and books with one another, that the meaning of reading lies. Choosing to encourage such reading may also be considered a political act.

<hr/>

Years later I read Janice A. Radway's *Reading the Romance: Women, Patriarchy, and Popular Literature*. This book caught my notice at two vastly different stages of my recent career. The first was in graduate school when a friend who knew of my romance/confession writing lent me his copy of Radway's book. Consumed by required reading, required papers, and freshman-composition students, I had to return the book unread. When, years later, my husband came across an APA-style reference to the book that indicated only the author's initials, he expressed frustration over not knowing the author's gender. I recognized the title and supplied the author's name.

Shortly thereafter, a colleague at the university of my first full-time employment heard of the encyclopedia project and offered to lend me a new edition of Radway's book. My path seemed fated to cross Radway's. So even though the encyclopedia was not to include, other than by brief mention, Radway's topic of popular romance, I decided to peruse at least her introduction. Part of my curiosity included a desire to clarify connections between the classically defined Romance tale and what my editor termed its stepsister.

My encyclopedia proposal wings its way to the requested outside reader, a woman chosen by my editor; she has completed many projects for him in the past. She is not an academic, nor is her last name Collins or Jong. My pride inflates as I read in her response, "On the surface, this well-appointed proposal tends to sway my approval. In fact, its punctilious style and word count puts my efforts at proposal-writing to shame." Then comes the shock: "However, I feel that the intended coverage is deficient in the current feminist . . . market." My indignation caused me to assume a who-are-you-to stance, and for a time, I simply thought she must be crazy. How could feminism possibly relate to romance? Had not I spent several painful years using feminist ideas specifically to reveal the weaknesses in my romantic ideology? Up to my newly liberated eyeballs in feminist ideology, I remained momentarily blind to her point.

When I recover from my shock, I take time to absorb her suggestions, many of which I find astute and useful: "To the list I would add miscegenation and rape and violence. . . . Slavery would make a worthy topic. . . . To the 1,000-word essays I would add patriarchal marriage—and place it in a starring role." Yes, I think. Yes, indeed.

Concisely and systematically she moves down my list, and in three pages offers suggestions for further deletions and additions.

She concludes with "This work has real possibilities," commenting again on my need for "meatier entries." My oversights I chalk up to a mixture of myopia and denial, still present at this late stage in my career. I pick and choose from among her suggestions and compose a final head-word list.

My contract arrives two weeks later.

Before long, my older daughter delivers additional copies of critical and review material on various of my selections, including more information on Naipaul. I'm especially intrigued by Naipaul's comments in an interview with Aamer Hussein regarding his latest book on India, *India: A Million Mutinies Now,* which he claims

> "is not an oral history; it's an account of a civilization at a hinge moment. It's done through human experience; there's a special shape to the book, it's held together by a thread of inquiry. . . . The idea came to me that the truth about India wasn't what I thought about India, it's what they [Indians] are living through. That is the great discovery; I moved to it slowly through earlier books, the books about the Islamic countries and the Deep South. I arrived at that form in the South, when people were describing to me what they felt; I was so excited by what I discovered. I'd never known about music and religion as supports against anarchy. I'd never understood it." (qtd. Hussein, 3)

I readily identify with his discovery. The use of the metanarrative of religion to keep the Other in its place I know well. Advantaged by familiarity with its author's thoughts almost forty years after its creation, I turn again to Naipaul's *Elvira.* If no romantic theme exists, perhaps I will catch a glimpse of a postmodern attitude toward the subject simply through an *absence* of traditional ideas of Romance. That would offer a statement of sorts.

The Suffrage of Elvira, a political/social-concerns novel, does not devote much space to images of affection. The plot focuses on a political election in the small Trinidadian town of Elvira, where struggles ensue between Muslim and Hindu factions. This is a truly entertaining novel. It frames a serious subject in humor and satire, both emphasized by the dialect in which the characters converse. Naipaul's seeming message that traditions of religion prevent intellectual advancement can be interpreted as possessing the seeds of postmodern ideas.

Two different subplots yield promise for my discussion of romance. In one, a nameless daughter-in-law, deserted by her husband, who never appears in the novel, acts as a servant to her in-laws. Her father-in-law addresses her only by a title, *doolahin,* indicating her married relationship to his son, as he orders her about. He refers euphemistically to his son's desertion of his spousal responsibility as a quest for education; the son left for school in Europe. The *doolahin,* after two years of service and obviously unhappy with the arrangement, appears to lack a solution to her conundrum. In another subplot, a young Hindu girl has become a pawn for her father in a marriage he hopes to arrange with the son of the wealthy political Hindu figure for whom the father campaigns. This son also remains absent from the novel; he's never seen or heard from. The girl, Nellie Chittaranjan, confides to a young Muslim friend, Foam Baksh, that she does not wish to marry, but instead desires to attend the Regent Street Polytechnic in London. A witness sees her speaking with Foam and circulates the unjust rumor that she, a Hindu, is keeping company with a Muslim. On the basis of this information, her father confines her to her home. I immediately think of Edmund Spenser's Blatant Beast, that symbol of Slander that could slay, simply through language, the purest of maidens.

Not even a single scene of hand-holding appears in the novel, although the narrative hints at some physical contact between Lorkhoor, the town rogue (a writer, of course), and a mysterious female companion. It lacks romance in the traditional sense of the term, but an idea begins to take shape in my mind. I think of Romance as a quest, as forces working together to defeat conflict. I think of a community united through gender interests or oppression or love or . . . I picture Nellie Chittaranjan, dreaming not of a young man, but of an education and a career. I picture the *doolahin,* valued only for her physical service, undeserving of even a name. And my idea percolates.

From its first page, the Radway book fascinates me. I spend several hours digesting her introduction. I learn that the subject of the popular romance came to her in graduate school from her dissertation studies of the differences between "elite" and "popular" literature. She notes that after taking part in a "feminist consciousness-raising group," she followed up on a curiosity centered on feminist writing, hoping to join her developing feminist "personal" interests to her "supposedly nongendered academic work" (6). She tells of having been hired due to her background work in popular literature by an institution that had, in the late seventies, begun critically "to elaborate on the assumption that works selected on the basis of their aesthetic achievement would necessarily be representative of the large sections of the population that had never read such books" (3). Her book will focus on just such a population, a group of popular-romance readers in a Midwestern city she calls Smithton. Part of her theory involved readers attaching to texts a semiotic, or symbolic, importance because of something other than just the stories they tell.

Radway's account of an increase in "politicization" growing from her personal identification with her all-female subjects also mentions the resultant parallels she drew to feminist studies being carried out in Britain. These studies helped shape her ability to analyze what determined women's situations in a material and social context. She writes,

Since I was assuming from the start with reader theorist
Stanley Fish that interpretations are constructed by interpretive communities using specific interpretive strategies, I
sought to contrast the then-current interpretation of romances produced by trained literary critics with that produced by fans of the genre. Thus, in going into the field, I
still conceived of reading in a limited fashion as interpretation and saw the project largely as one focusing on the dif-
ferential interpretation of texts. It was only when the
Smithton women repeatedly answered my questions about
the meaning of romances by talking about the meaning of
romance reading as an activity and a social event in a fa-
milial context that the study began to intersect with work
being done in Britain. (7)

Her discussions with her subjects prompted their consistent and
voluntary reference to a "connection between their reading and
their daily social situation as wives and mothers," leading Radway to resort to feminist-theoretical explanatory concepts, such
as that of patriarchal marriage. This not only aided in her accounting for the "social situation" in which the reading occurred
but also allowed her to apply Nancy Chodorow's psychoanalytic
theories "to explain the construction of desire responsible for
their [the romance-reading women] location and their partial dissatisfaction with it, which itself leads ultimately to repetitive romance reading" (9).

Chodorow's ideas encouraged Radway to envision the appeal
of an ultramasculine, yet nurturing, romantic hero character as
part of the romance-reading female's search to regain the nurturing provided by her mother. The romance reader, usually a wife
and mother herself, constantly nurtured others, but no one nurtured her. This helped explain the seeming contradiction in the
fact that the readers chose to identify with a character/heroine
caught up in the very type of heterosexual relationship they found
so lacking in their own lives. Radway's idea of a nurturing hero

reminds me of a comment from a writer of popular romance at a recent writer's conference: "Today's young men should read our romances as how-to guides."

Interesting discoveries from Radway's study in Smithton included the women's definite delight in being part of a "large exclusively female community" made up of readers who all frequented the same bookstore for advice about book choice from the nationally recognized romance "expert" who worked at the store. This expert tells Radway that she "believes a good romance focuses on an intelligent and able heroine who finds a man who recognizes her special qualities and is capable of loving and caring for her as she wants to be loved. [She] understands such an ending to say that female independence and marriage are compatible rather than mutually exclusive" (54). Also intriguing was the way in which the women saw their reading as a way to temporarily duck the demands of their domestic scene. They established a physical perimeter that said to their family members, "Leave me alone. I'm reading." The act of reading itself was viewed as a "declaration of independence" (11). One might even label it, then, a political act.

Another critic comments regarding readers of du Maurier's *Rebecca*, with its Byronic hero and decidedly unconventional (s)hero. Alison Light disputes the stereotypical picture of the "mindless" romance reader in so far as it treats women "yet again as the victims of, and irrational slaves to, their sensibilities," a view she calls a denigrating product of "puritanical Left-wing moralism." According to Light, feminists should question any conclusion implying stupidity or masochism in connection with romance readers. Such reading might even convert its reader to feminism: "reading is never simply a linear con-job but a process of interaction . . . a process which helps to query as well as endorse social meanings and one which therefore remains dynamic and open to change" (8). She concludes that women's reading of romance is "as much a measure of their deep dissatisfaction with heterosexual options as of any desire to be fully identified with the submissive versions of femininity the texts endorse. Romance imagines peace, security and ease precisely because there is dissension, insecurity and difficulty" (22).

My investigation of Radway's conclusions and Light's ideas regarding the dynamic nature of reading informs my view of the place of traditional Romance in a postmodern world. Thoughts of all selves revising, re-calling, through language, old ideas by new names, helps me envision today's and tomorrow's readers turning to yesterday's fiction for knowledge helpful to their formation of self-concept. This idea of the active and interactive reading individual, regardless of subject matter, remains crucial to literary criticism of a feminist bent. Light writes that the recognition of subjectivity in the reading and writing practice does not force a "retreat into 'subjectivisim.'" It offers instead the recognition that "any feminist literary critical enterprise" asks questions of social and historical institutions resulting from cultural formations, "not just as they operate 'out there,' but as they inform and structure the material 'in there'—the identities through which we live, and which may allow us to become the agents of political change" (23).

⚜

I turn back to *Elvira,* and discover to my delight that the *doolahin* has run away from the oppressive atmosphere of their village with the n'er-do-well Lorkhoor. She rebels, leaving a marriage to a nonexistent husband and a life of slavery to his father, refusing to participate in their traditional patriarchal discourse. She strikes up a relationship on her own terms with a man who for once symbolizes freedom rather than oppression. I find Nellie Chittaranjan freed by the very slander that threatened further to imprison her. The father of the high-standing Hindu boy uses rumors of Nelly's supposed forbidden rendezvous with a Muslim as an excuse to deny her the privilege of marrying his son. Nellie departs Elvira for London and the Polytechnic, enjoying the bounty of her own suffrage, abandoning tradition in a manner every bit as revolutionary as that of the *doolahin,* whose story acts as Nellie's cautionary tale.

Nellie and the *doolahin* indeed remain a part of an adventure, a Romance if you will, composed of magical and imaginative events. They symbolize their own readers, individuals ready to re-imagine, re-vision, re-create their private selves, wooed through a language of freedom. It's Byron's vision and our own, a chance to balance the metaphysical and the ironic, creating a positive ethics promoted by literature that finds a conduit for release through each individual reader. That private reader and the public community of readers to which she/he belongs complement one another, resisting a reductionist vision to any single viewpoint regarding the pathway to Truth. The decision to stop searching for the/a Truth in any one metanarrative to which we cling requires a courage, a (s)heroism that will also serve to bridge the gap between our past and our newly alienated selves. It's all about reading and language and sharing with, not forcing upon, others the ideas we treasure.

Waugh writes that "much contemporary feminist fictional writing . . . has accommodated humanist beliefs in individual agency and the necessity and possibility of self-reflection and historical continuity as the basis for personal identity." In addition, it "modifies traditional beliefs," emphasizing their "provisionality and positionality" in matters "of identity, the historical and social construction of gender, and the discursive production of knowledge and power" (13). These newer texts seem to legitimize a continuous interaction with the old, suggesting the possibility that one may see one's self acting with strength, "as a coherent agent in the world, at the same time as understanding the extent to which identity and gender are socially constructed and represented" (13).

A few months earlier, I had received an e-mail both amusing and informative from my then-college freshperson daughter, enrolled at the University of Missouri. It serves to illustrate the effects of sharing our favored writings and stories. She writes of her English teacher, who

> used to read Socrates and Confucius to her girls because she doesn't like fairytales and animal stories make her cry. Also, they were only allowed to speak Spanish on Monday, German on Tuesday, Italian on Wednesday, French on Thursday, and Gaelic on Friday, and English was for the weekends. . . . All I have to say is thank you for reading me Snow White; I like it fine.

Creating and sharing our own literary traditions within the circle of individuals most important to us remains crucial. This situation perhaps flies in the face of postmodern ideas and their offspring, deconstructive criticism. But those approaches seem to contain the seeds of their own future self-immolation in their rejection of tradition as a tool for reaping knowledge. For me, what may be salvaged from these approaches to knowledge remains the emphasis on the constant emergence of new visions from age-old experience and their encouragement of the formation of small communities made up of individuals who share common interests. The next generation will re-vision classic ideas of (R/r)omance as it needs—as it must.

Notes

CHAPTER ONE

1. From the State Paper Office, Domestic, Charles I, an excerpt from a letter written to Lord Conway by Elizabeth Tanfield Cary, Lady Falkland. See the appendix in Simpson's *The Lady Falkland: Her Life from a ms. in the Imperial Archives at Lille* (London: Catholic Publishing & Bookselling, 1861), 144.

2. Donald Stauffer, "A Deep and Sad Passion," *Essays in Dramatic Literature: The Parrot Presentation Volume,* ed. Hardin Craig (Princeton: Princeton University Press, 1935), 289–314.

3. In 1994 a long-awaited new edition of Cary's play and her biography edited by Barry Weller and Margaret Ferguson, *The Tragedy of Mariam: The Fair Queen of Jewry with The Lady Falkland: Her Life: by One of her Daughters* (Berkeley: University of California Press) appeared. This version does not, however, contain the Carys' personal correspondence, found in an appendix in the Simpson volume, from which I quote in this essay.

4. The works I consult the most closely are Drayton's *The Barons Warres; Englands Heroicall Epistles: Queene Isabel to Mortimer;* and "The Legend of Pierce Gaveston" from *The Works of Michael Drayton* (Oxford: Shakespeare Head Press, 1931).

5. See Virginia Brackett's "Elizabeth Cary, Drayton, and Edward II," *Notes and Queries* 41.4 (December 1994): 517–19.

CHAPTER THREE

1. I choose not to identify the editors from whose personal correspondence I quote.

CHAPTER FIVE

1. I choose not to identify the editors from whose personal correspondence I quote.

Works Cited

Atkins, G. Douglas, and Michael L. Johnson, eds. *Writing and Reading Differently: Deconstruction and the Teaching of Composition and Literature.* Lawrence: University Press of Kansas, 1985.

Atkins, G. Douglas, and Michael L. Johnson. Introduction to *Writing and Reading Differently: Deconstruction and the Teaching of Composition and Literature,* 1–14. Lawrence: University Press of Kansas, 1985.

Atkins, G. Douglas. *Estranging the Familiar: Toward a Revitalized Critical Writing.* Athens: University of Georgia Press, 1992.

Barringer, Robby. "Position Paper: Richard Rorty's 'Private Irony and Liberal Hope." 2 April 1996. 2 June 1997. <http://www. english.udel.edu/gweight/prof/web/rorty2.html>.

———. "Rorty's Language Theory Applied to Literary Theory." n.d. 2 June 1997. <http://www.english.udel.edu/teague/barringer1. html>.

Bradstreet, Anne. *The Complete Works of Anne Bradstreet.* Edited by Joseph R. McElrath, Jr. and Allan P. Robb. Boston: Twayne, 1981.

———. *The Works of Anne Bradstreet.* Edited by Jeanine Hensley. Cambridge: Harvard University Press, 1967.

Bressler, Charles E., ed. *Literary Criticism: An Introduction to Theory and Practice.* Englewood Cliffs: Prentice Hall, 1994.

Brown, Ellen. "Between the Medusa and the Abyss: Reading *Jane Eyre,* Reading Myself." In *The Intimate Critique: Autobiographical Literary Criticism,* edited by Diane P. Freedman, Olivia Frey, and Frances Murphy Zauhar, 225–35. Durham: Duke University Press, 1993.

161

Byron, George Gordon Lord. "Don Juan." In *Byron*, edited by Jerome J. McGann. New York: Oxford University Press, 1986.

Carlton, Peter. "Rereading Middlemarch, Rereading Myself." In *The Intimate Critique: Autobiographical Literary Criticism*, edited by Diane P. Freedman, Olivia Frey, and Frances Murphy Zauhar, 237–244. Durham: Duke University Press, 1993.

Cary, Elizabeth Tanfield. *The History of the Life, Reign, and Death of Edward II, King of England and Lord of Ireland with the Rise and Fall of His Great Favourites, Gaveston and the Spencers*. London: J.C. for Charles Harper et al., 1680.

———. *The Tragedie of Mariam, Faire Queene of Jewry*. Edited by A.C. Dunstan, 1613. London: Thomas Creede for Richard Hawkins; London: Oxford University Press, 1914.

Cary, Elizabeth. *The Tragedy of Mariam the Fair Queen of Jewry*. Edited by Berry Weller and Margaret W. Ferguson. 1613. *The Tragedy of Mariam the Fair Queen of Jewry with The Lady Falkland her Life by One of her Daughters*. Berkeley: University of California Press, 1994, 65–176.

Cixous, Hélène. "Castration or Decapitation?" Translated by Annette Kuhn. *Signs: Journal of Women in Culture and Society* 7.11 (1981): 41–55.

Davis, Natalie Zemon. "Women on Top: Symbolic Sexual Inversion and Political Disorder in Early Modern Europe." In *Society and Culture in Early Modern France: Eight Essays* by Natalie Zemon Davis. Stanford: Stanford University Press, 1975.

DuPlessis, Rachel Blau. *The Pink Guitar: Writing as Feminist Practice*. New York: Routledge, 1990.

Foucault, Michel. *The Care of the Self: The History of Sexuality*. Translated by Robert Hurley. Volume 3. New York: Random House, 1988.

———. *The Care of the Self: The History of Sexuality*. Translated by Robert Hurley. Volume I: *An Introduction*. 1976. New York: Random House, 1978.

Freedman, Diane P., Olivia Frey, and Frances Murphy Zauhar, eds. *The Intimate Critique: Autobiographical Literary Criticism*. Durham: Duke University Press, 1993.

Freedman, Diane P., Olivia Frey, and Frances Murphy Zauhar. Introduction to *The Intimate Critique: Autobiographical Literary*

Criticism, edited by Diane P. Freedman, Olivia Frey, and Frances Murphy Zauhar, 1–10. Durham: Duke University Press, 1993.

Frey, Olivia. "Beyond Literary Darwinism: Women's Voices and Critical Discourse." In *The Intimate Critique: Autobiographical Literary Criticism,* edited by Diane P. Freedman, Olivia Frey, and Frances Murphy Zauhar, 41–63. Durham: Duke University Press, 1993.

Gallop, Jane. "Forum." *PMLA* 111.5 (October 1996): 1149–50.

Gardiner, Judith. "On Female Identity and Writing by Women." *Writing and Sexual Difference,* edited by Elizabeth Abel, 177–91. Chicago: University of Chicago Press, 1980.

Gilman, Charlotte Perkins. "The Yellow Wallpaper." In *Responding to Literature,* edited by Judith A. Stanford, 2nd ed., 575–87. Mountain View, Calif.: Mayfield, 1996.

———. "Why I Wrote 'The Yellow Wallpaper.'" In *Responding to Literature,* edited by Judith A. Stanford, 2nd ed., 589–90. Mountain View, Calif.: Mayfield, 1996.

Haselkorn, Anne M., and Betty S. Travitsky, eds. *The Renaissance Englishwoman in Print: Counterbalancing the Canon.* Amherst: University of Massachusetts Press, 1990.

Henderson, Katherine Usher, and Barbara F. McManus. *Half Humankind: Contexts and Texts of the Controversy about Women in England, 1540–1640.* Urbana: University of Illinois Press, 1985.

"History of Allegheny College." 15 September 1997. 23 February 1998. <http://www.alleg.edu/Info/History.html>.

Hughes, Merritt Y., ed. *John Milton: Complete Poems and Major Prose.* New York: Macmillan, 1957.

Hussein, Aamer. "Delivering the Truth: An Interview with V. S. Naipaul." *Times Literary Supplement,* 2 September 1994, 3–4.

Index of Dedications and Commendatory Verses in English Books before 1641. Edited by Franklin B. Williams, Jr. London: The Bibliographical Society, 1962.

Jordan, Constance. *Renaissance Feminism: Literary Texts and Political Models.* Ithaca: Cornell University Press, 1990.

Kaufer, David, and Gary Waller. "To Write Is to Read Is to Write, Right?" In *Writing and Reading Differently: Deconstruction and the Teaching of Composition and Literature,* edited by

G. Douglas Atkins and Michael L. Johnson, 66–92. Lawrence: University Press of Kansas, 1985.

Krontiris, Tina. "Style and Gender in Elizabeth Cary's Edward II." In *The Renaissance Englishwoman in Print: Counterbalancing the Canon,* edited by Anne M. Haselkorn and Betty S. Travitsky, 137–53. Amherst: University of Massachusetts Press, 1990.

Kübler-Ross, Elizabeth. "On the Fear of Death." In *Responding to Literature,* edited by Judith A. Stanford, 2nd ed., 1200–1206. Mountain View, Calif.: Mayfield, 1996.

Leitch, Vincent B. "Deconstruction and Pedagogy." In *Writing and Reading Differently: Deconstruction and the Teaching of Composition and Literature,* edited by G. Douglas Atkins and Michael L. Johnson, 16–26. Lawrence: University Press of Kansas, 1985.

Lewalski, Barbara Keifer. "Resisting Tyrants: Elizabeth Cary's Tragedy and History." In *Writing Women in Jacobean England,* 179–211. Cambridge: Harvard University Press, 1993.

Light, Alison. "'Returning to Manderley': Romance Fiction, Female Sexuality and Class." *Feminist Review* 16 (April 1984): 7–25.

Lyotard, Jean-François. *The Postmodern Condition.* Minneapolis: University of Minnesota Press, 1984.

Martin, Wendy. *An American Triptych: Anne Bradstreet, Emily Dickinson, Adrienne Rich.* Chapel Hill: University of North Carolina Press, 1984.

McHale, Brian. *Postmodernist Fiction.* New York: Methuen, 1987.

McLaughlin, Janice. "Feminist Relations with Postmodernism." *Journal of Gender Studies* 6.1 (March 1997): 5–15.

McNay, Lois. *Foucault and Feminism: Power, Gender, and the Self.* Boston: Northeastern University Press, 1992.

Millay, Edna St. Vincent. "[The courage that my mother had]." In *The Norton Anthology of Literature by Women: Traditions in English,* edited by Sandra M. Gilbert and Susan Gubar, 1568. New York: Norton, 1985.

Miller, Nancy K. *Getting Personal: Feminist Occasions and Other Autobiographical Acts.* New York: Routledge, 1991.

Milton, John. "Aeropagitica." 1644. In *John Milton: Complete Poems and Major Prose,* edited by Merritt Y. Hughes, 716–49. New York: Macmillan, 1957.

———. "L'Allegro." *John Milton: Complete Poems and Major Prose*, edited by Merritt Y. Hughes, 68–72. New York: Macmillan, 1957.

Mitchell, Margaret. *Gone with the Wind*. Garden City, N.Y.: International Collectors Library, 1964.

Mourad, Roger P. "Richard Rorty." *Review of Higher Education* 20.2 (1997): 113–40.

Porter, Katherine Anne. "The Jilting of Granny Weatherall." In *Responding to Literature*, edited by Judith A. Stanford, 2nd ed., 1124–31. Mountain View, Calif.: Mayfield, 1996.

Pritchard, William H. "Naipaul's Written World." *Hudson Review* (Winter 1995): 587–96.

Radway, Janice A. *Reading the Romance: Women, Patriarchy, and Popular Literature*. 1984. Chapel Hill: University of North Carolina Press, 1991.

Roche, Thomas P., Jr., ed. *The Faerie Queene*. 1590. New York: Penguin, 1978.

Rorty, Richard. "The Dangers of Over-Philosophication—Reply to Arcilla and Nicholson." *Educational Theory* 40.1 (Winter 1990): 41–44.

———. *Consequences of Pragmatism: (Essays 1972–1980)*. Minneapolis: University of Minnesota Press, 1982.

———. *Contingency, Irony, and Solidarity*. New York: Cambridge University Press, 1989.

Rothfork, John. "Postmodern Ethics: Richard Rorty & Michael Polanyi." *Southern Humanities Review* 29.1 (1995): 15–48.

Rousseau, Jean-Jacques. 1762. "*Emile*: Selections." Translated by William Boyd. Edited by William Boyd. New York: Teachers College Press: Columbia University, 1970.

Shakespeare, William. "*The Tragedy of Macbeth*." In *The Riverside Shakespeare*, edited by G. Blakemore Evans et al., 1306–42. Boston: Houghton Mifflin, 1974.

Simpson, Richard, ed. *The Lady Falkland: Her Life from a ms. in the Imperial Archives at Lille*. London: Catholic Publishing & Bookselling, 1861.

Spivak, Gayatri Chakravorty. "Reading the World: Literary Studies in the 1980s." In *Writing and Reading Differently: Deconstruction and the Teaching of Composition and Literature*, edited by

G. Douglas Atkins and Michael L. Johnson, 27–37. Lawrence: University Press of Kansas, 1985.

Stanford, Judith A., ed. *Responding to Literature.* 2nd ed. Mountain View, Calif.: Mayfield, 1996.

Stauffer, Donald. "A Deep and Sad Passion." In *Essays in Dramatic Literature: The Parrot Presentation Volume,* edited by Hardin Craig, 289–314. Princeton: Princeton University Press, 1935.

Tagore, Rabindranath. "Fruit Gathering." In *Responding to Literature,* edited by Judith A. Stanford, 2nd ed., 1200. Mountain View, Calif.: Mayfield, 1996.

The Arte of English Poesie. 1589. Edited by Edward Arber. Amsterdam: De Capo Press, 1971.

The Lady Falkland her Life by One of her Daughters. Edited by Berry Weller and Margaret W. Ferguson. *The Tragedy of Mariam the Fair Queen of Jewry with The Lady Falkland her Life by One of her Daughters.* Berkeley: University of California Press, 1994. 183–275.

Thorne, Barrie, and Nancy Henley, eds. *Language and Sex: Difference and Dominance.* Rowley, Mass.: Newbury House, 1975.

Tierney, William G. "Border Crossings: Critical Theory and the Study of Higher Education." In *Culture and Ideology in Higher Education: Advancing a Critical Agenda,* edited by William G. Tierney, 3–15. New York: Praeger, 1991.

Tolstoy, Leo. *Anna Karenina.* 1878. New York: Norton, 1970.

Tompkins, Jane. "Me and My Shadow." In *The Intimate Critique: Autobiographical Literary Criticism,* edited by Diane P. Freedman, Olivia Frey, and Frances Murphy Zauhar, 23–40. Durham: Duke University Press, 1993.

Travitsky, Betty S. "The Feme Covert in Elizabeth Cary's Mariam." In *Ambiguous Realities: Women in the Middle Ages and Renaissance,* edited by Carole Levin and Jeanie Watson, 184–96. Detroit: Wayne State University Press, 1987.

Usher, Robin, and Richard Edwards. *Postmodernism and Education.* London: Routledge, 1994.

Waugh, Patricia. *Feminine Fictions: Revisiting the Postmodern.* New York: Routledge, 1989.

Weller, Berry, and Margaret W. Ferguson, eds. *The Tragedy of Mariam the Fair Queen of Jewry with The Lady Falkland her Life by One of her Daughters.* Berkeley: University of California Press, 1994.

Whiteis, David G. "Finding Inspiration in Literature." *The Chronicle of Higher Education,* March 8, 1996, B4.

Williams, Aubrey, ed. *Poetry and Prose of Alexander Pope.* Boston: Houghton Mifflin, 1969.

Winthrop, John. *Winthrop's Journal: "History of New England":* *1630–1649.* Edited by James Kendall Hosmer. *Original Narratives of Early American History,* vol. 2. New York: Barnes & Noble, 1908.

Woolf, Virginia. *A Writer's Diary.* New York: Harcourt, Brace, 1954.

Zauhar, Frances Murphy. "Creative Voices: Women Reading and Women's Writing." In *The Intimate Critique: Autobiographical Literary Criticism,* edited by Diane P. Freedman, Olivia Frey, and Frances Murphy Zauhar, 103–16. Durham: Duke University Press, 1993.

Index

Edward II, King, 5, 21, 37, 85, 159n.5
Edwards, Richard, 61–62
Egoist, The (Meredith), 81
Elizabeth I, Queen, 88, 90
Emile (Rousseau), 52
Enemies: A Love Story (Singer), 136
episteme/epistomology, 6, 18–20, 130, 141
Estefan, Gloria, 46
Eyre, Jane, 126–27

Fairie Queene, The (Spenser), 79
feminism/feminist theory, 1, 5, 14,17, 20, 24, 29, 30, 44, 50–51, 83, 127, 138–39, 142, 156; and postmodernism, 6, 10–13, 80, 121, 129–32; and Romance, 120, 123, 149, 152–55; and writing, 6, 9–10, 18–19, 49, 73–74, 80, 133. *See also* Atkins, G. Douglas; Chodorow, Nancy; Freedman, Diane P.; Frey, Olivia; Gardiner, Judith; Jordan, Constance; Lewalski, Barbara Keifer; Martin, Wendy; McLaughlin, Janice; McNay, Lois; Miller, Nancy; Spivak, Gayatri Chakravorty; Steinem, Gloria; Tompkins, Jane; Travitsky, Betty; Waugh, Patricia
Ferguson, Margaret. Work: *The Tragedy of Mariam: the Fair Queen of Jewry,* ed., 78, 159n.3

Fish, Stanley, 153
Foucault, Michel, 6, 48–49, 62, 64, 130
Freedman, Diane P., 77
French Revolution, 138
Freud, Sigmund, 9–10
Frey, Olivia, 18, 72–74
"Fruit Gathering" (Tagore), 113–16

Galen, 24, 48
Gallop, Jane, 75
Gardiner, Judith, 28
Gilman, Charlotte Perkins, 41, 54, 67. Works: "The Yellow Wallpaper," 41–44, 52–54, 67; "Why I Wrote 'The Yellow Wallpaper'," 67
Glaspell, Susan, 87
Gluckel of Hameln, 91
Gone with the Wind (Mitchell), 123, 125–26

Hammett, Dashiell. Work: *Woman in the Dark,* 81
Hand Maid's Tale, The (Atwood), 136
Heathcliffe, 125
Henderson, Katherine Usher. Work: *Half Humankind: Contexts and Texts of the Controversy about Women in England, 1540–1640,* 78
Henley, Nancy. Work: *Language and Sex: Difference and Dominance,* 78
Henrietta Maria, Queen, 39–40

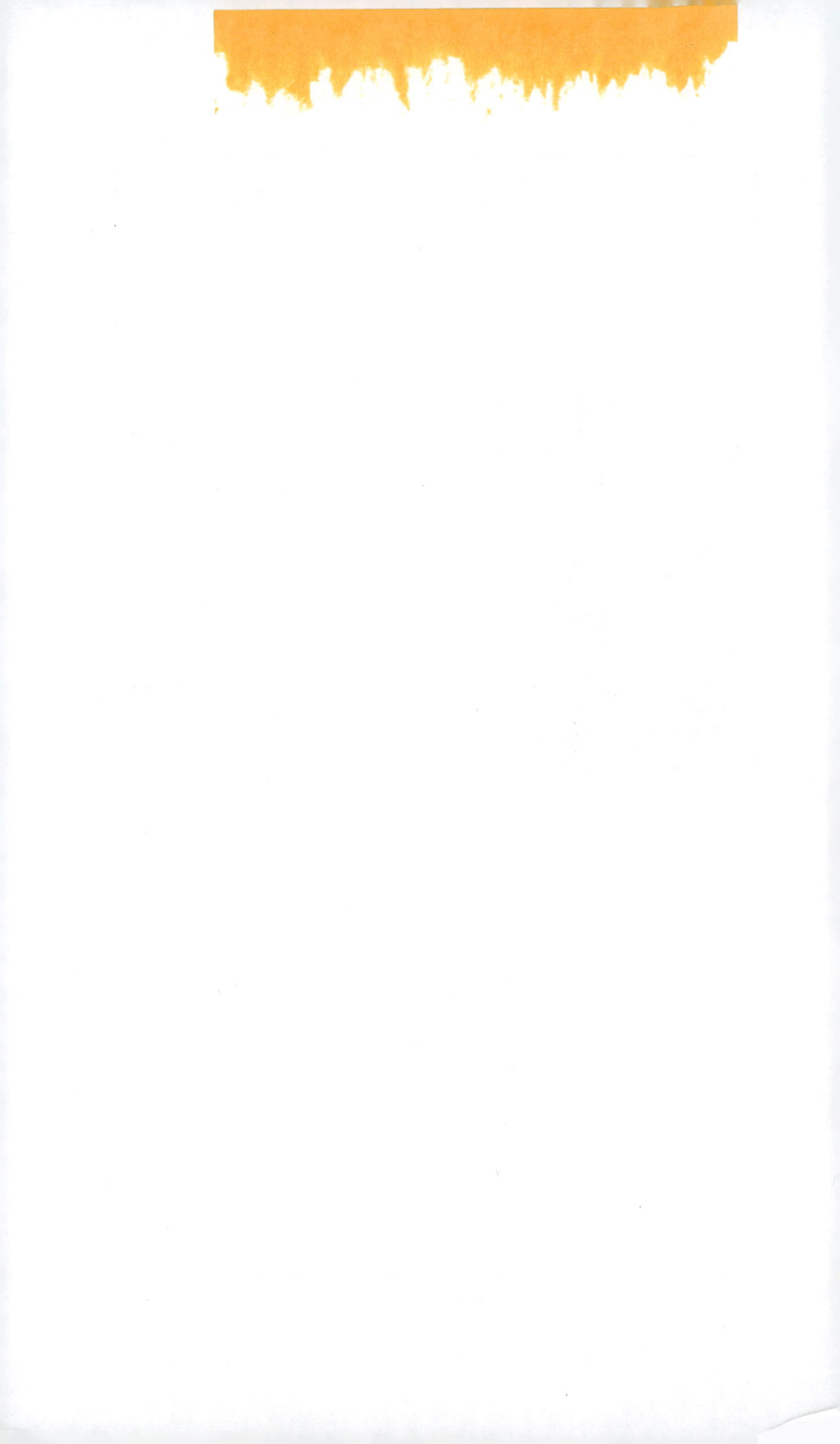